BENJAMIN FRANKLIN

WORLD LEADERS PAST & PRESENT

BENJAMIN FRANKLIN

Chris Looby

CHELSEA HOUSE PUBLISHERS
NEW YORK
PHILADELPHIA

Chelsea House Publishers
EDITOR-IN-CHIEF: Nancy Toff
EXECUTIVE EDITOR: Remmel T. Nunn
MANAGING EDITOR: Karyn Gullen Browne
COPY CHIEF: Juliann Barbato
PICTURE EDITOR: Adrian G. Allen
ART DIRECTOR: Maria Epes
MANUFACTURING MANAGER: Gerald Levine

World Leaders—Past & Present
SENIOR EDITOR: John W. Selfridge

Staff for BENJAMIN FRANKLIN
ASSISTANT EDITOR: Terrance Dolan
DEPUTY COPY CHIEF: Nicole Bowen
EDITORIAL ASSISTANT: Nate Eaton
PICTURE RESEARCHER: Lisa Kirchner
ASSISTANT ART DIRECTOR: Loraine Machlin
ASSISTANT DESIGNER: James Baker
PRODUCTION MANAGER: Joseph Romano
PRODUCTION COORDINATOR: Marie Claire Cebrián
COVER ILLUSTRATION: Ken Christie

3 5 7 9 8 6 4 2

Library of Congress Cataloging-in-Publication Data

Looby, Chris.
Benjamin Franklin / Chris Looby.
p. cm.—(World leaders past & present)
Includes bibliographical references.
Summary: Examines the life of the noted statesman who was accomplished in many fields.
ISBN 1-55546-808-X
0-7910-0695-6 (pbk.)
1. Franklin. Benjamin, 1706–1790—Juvenile literature.
2. Statesmen—United States—Biography—Juvenile literature.
3. Printers—United States—Biography—Juvenile literature.
4. Scientists—United States—Biography—Juvenile literature.
[1. Franklin, Benjamin, 1706–1790. 2. Statesmen.] I. Title.
II. Series.
E302.6.F8L77 1990
973.3'092—dc20 89–38478
[B] CIP
[92] AC

Contents

"On Leadership," Arthur M. Schlesinger, jr. 7

1. Hanging Together 13
2. A Rational Creature 27
3. Poor Richard 37
4. "A House Thus Furnished" 49
5. Cool Thoughts 61
6. An American Patriot in London 73
7. An American Patriot in Paris 87
8. The Public Good 99

Further Reading 108

Chronology 109

Index 110

John Adams
John Quincy Adams
Konrad Adenauer
Alexander the Great
Salvador Allende
Marc Antony
Corazon Aquino
Yasir Arafat
King Arthur
Hafez al-Assad
Kemal Atatürk
Attila
Clement Attlee
Augustus Caesar
Menachem Begin
David Ben-Gurion
Otto von Bismarck
Léon Blum
Simon Bolívar
Cesare Borgia
Willy Brandt
Leonid Brezhnev
Julius Caesar
John Calvin
Jimmy Carter
Fidel Castro
Catherine the Great
Charlemagne
Chiang Kai-Shek
Winston Churchill
Georges Clemenceau
Cleopatra
Constantine the Great
Hernán Cortés
Oliver Cromwell
Georges-Jacques Danton
Jefferson Davis
Moshe Dayan
Charles de Gaulle
Eamon De Valera
Eugene Debs
Deng Xiaoping
Benjamin Disraeli
Alexander Dubček
François & Jean-Claude Duvalier
Dwight Eisenhower
Eleanor of Aquitaine
Elizabeth I
Faisal
Ferdinand & Isabella
Francisco Franco
Benjamin Franklin
Frederick the Great
Indira Gandhi
Mohandas Gandhi
Giuseppe Garibaldi
Amin & Bashir Gemayel
Genghis Khan
William Gladstone
Mikhail Gorbachev
Ulysses S. Grant
Ernesto "Che" Guevara
Tenzin Gyatso
Alexander Hamilton
Dag Hammarskjöld
Henry VIII
Henry of Navarre
Paul von Hindenburg
Hirohito
Adolf Hitler
Ho Chi Minh
King Hussein
Ivan the Terrible
Andrew Jackson
James I
Wojciech Jaruzelski
Thomas Jefferson
Joan of Arc
Pope John XXIII
Pope John Paul II
Lyndon Johnson
Benito Juárez
John Kennedy
Robert Kennedy
Jomo Kenyatta
Ayatollah Khomeini
Nikita Khrushchev
Kim Il Sung
Martin Luther King, Jr.
Henry Kissinger
Kublai Khan
Lafayette
Robert E. Lee
Vladimir Lenin
Abraham Lincoln
David Lloyd George
Louis XIV
Martin Luther
Judas Maccabeus
James Madison
Nelson & Winnie Mandela
Mao Zedong
Ferdinand Marcos
George Marshall
Mary, Queen of Scots
Tomáš Masaryk
Golda Meir
Klemens von Metternich
James Monroe
Hosni Mubarak
Robert Mugabe
Benito Mussolini
Napoléon Bonaparte
Gamal Abdel Nasser
Jawaharlal Nehru
Nero
Nicholas II
Richard Nixon
Kwame Nkrumah
Daniel Ortega
Mohammed Reza Pahlavi
Thomas Paine
Charles Stewart Parnell
Pericles
Juan Perón
Peter the Great
Pol Pot
Muammar el-Qaddafi
Ronald Reagan
Cardinal Richelieu
Maximilien Robespierre
Eleanor Roosevelt
Franklin Roosevelt
Theodore Roosevelt
Anwar Sadat
Haile Selassie
Prince Sihanouk
Jan Smuts
Joseph Stalin
Sukarno
Sun Yat-sen
Tamerlane
Mother Teresa
Margaret Thatcher
Josip Broz Tito
Toussaint L'Ouverture
Leon Trotsky
Pierre Trudeau
Harry Truman
Queen Victoria
Lech Walesa
George Washington
Chaim Weizmann
Woodrow Wilson
Xerxes
Emiliano Zapata
Zhou Enlai

ON LEADERSHIP

Arthur M. Schlesinger, jr.

LEADERSHIP, it may be said, is really what makes the world go round. Love no doubt smooths the passage; but love is a private transaction between consenting adults. Leadership is a public transaction with history. The idea of leadership affirms the capacity of individuals to move, inspire, and mobilize masses of people so that they act together in pursuit of an end. Sometimes leadership serves good purposes, sometimes bad; but whether the end is benign or evil, great leaders are those men and women who leave their personal stamp on history.

Now, the very concept of leadership implies the proposition that individuals can make a difference. This proposition has never been universally accepted. From classical times to the present day, eminent thinkers have regarded individuals as no more than the agents and pawns of larger forces, whether the gods and goddesses of the ancient world or, in the modern era, race, class, nation, the dialectic, the will of the people, the spirit of the times, history itself. Against such forces, the individual dwindles into insignificance.

So contends the thesis of historical determinism. Tolstoy's great novel *War and Peace* offers a famous statement of the case. Why, Tolstoy asked, did millions of men in the Napoleonic Wars, denying their human feelings and their common sense, move back and forth across Europe slaughtering their fellows? "The war," Tolstoy answered, "was bound to happen simply because it was bound to happen." All prior history predetermined it. As for leaders, they, Tolstoy said, "are but the labels that serve to give a name to an end and, like labels, they have the least possible connection with the event." The greater the leader, "the more conspicuous the inevitability and the predestination of every act he commits." The leader, said Tolstoy, is "the slave of history."

Determinism takes many forms. Marxism is the determinism of class. Nazism the determinism of race. But the idea of men and women as the slaves of history runs athwart the deepest human instincts. Rigid determinism abolishes the idea of human freedom—

the assumption of free choice that underlies every move we make, every word we speak, every thought we think. It abolishes the idea of human responsibility, since it is manifestly unfair to reward or punish people for actions that are by definition beyond their control. No one can live consistently by any deterministic creed. The Marxist states prove this themselves by their extreme susceptibility to the cult of leadership.

More than that, history refutes the idea that individuals make no difference. In December 1931 a British politician crossing Park Avenue in New York City between 76th and 77th Streets around 10:30 P.M. looked in the wrong direction and was knocked down by an automobile—a moment, he later recalled, of a man aghast, a world aglare: "I do not understand why I was not broken like an eggshell or squashed like a gooseberry." Fourteen months later an American politician, sitting in an open car in Miami, Florida, was fired on by an assassin; the man beside him was hit. Those who believe that individuals make no difference to history might well ponder whether the next two decades would have been the same had Mario Constasino's car killed Winston Churchill in 1931 and Giuseppe Zangara's bullet killed Franklin Roosevelt in 1933. Suppose, in addition, that Adolf Hitler had been killed in the street fighting during the Munich *Putsch* of 1923 and that Lenin had died of typhus during World War I. What would the 20th century be like now?

For better or for worse, individuals do make a difference. "The notion that a people can run itself and its affairs anonymously," wrote the philosopher William James, "is now well known to be the silliest of absurdities. Mankind does nothing save through initiatives on the part of inventors, great or small, and imitation by the rest of us—these are the sole factors in human progress. Individuals of genius show the way, and set the patterns, which common people then adopt and follow."

Leadership, James suggests, means leadership in thought as well as in action. In the long run, leaders in thought may well make the greater difference to the world. But, as Woodrow Wilson once said, "Those only are leaders of men, in the general eye, who lead in action. . . . It is at their hands that new thought gets its translation into the crude language of deeds." Leaders in thought often invent in solitude and obscurity, leaving to later generations the tasks of imitation. Leaders in action—the leaders portrayed in this series—have to be effective in their own time.

And they cannot be effective by themselves. They must act in response to the rhythms of their age. Their genius must be adapted, in a phrase of William James's, "to the receptivities of the moment." Leaders are useless without followers. "There goes the mob," said the French politician hearing a clamor in the streets. "I am their leader. I must follow them." Great leaders turn the inchoate emotions of the mob to purposes of their own. They seize on the opportunities of their time, the hopes, fears, frustrations, crises, potentialities. They succeed when events have prepared the way for them, when the community is awaiting to be aroused, when they can provide the clarifying and organizing ideas. Leadership ignites the circuit between the individual and the mass and thereby alters history.

It may alter history for better or for worse. Leaders have been responsible for the most extravagant follies and most monstrous crimes that have beset suffering humanity. They have also been vital in such gains as humanity has made in individual freedom, religious and racial tolerance, social justice, and respect for human rights.

There is no sure way to tell in advance who is going to lead for good and who for evil. But a glance at the gallery of men and women in *World Leaders—Past and Present* suggests some useful tests.

One test is this: Do leaders lead by force or by persuasion? By command or by consent? Through most of history leadership was exercised by the divine right of authority. The duty of followers was to defer and to obey. "Theirs not to reason why / Theirs but to do and die." On occasion, as with the so-called enlightened despots of the 18th century in Europe, absolutist leadership was animated by humane purposes. More often, absolutism nourished the passion for domination, land, gold, and conquest and resulted in tyranny.

The great revolution of modern times has been the revolution of equality. The idea that all people should be equal in their legal condition has undermined the old structure of authority, hierarchy, and deference. The revolution of equality has had two contrary effects on the nature of leadership. For equality, as Alexis de Tocqueville pointed out in his great study *Democracy in America*, might mean equality in servitude as well as equality in freedom.

"I know of only two methods of establishing equality in the political world," Tocqueville wrote. "Rights must be given to every citizen, or none at all to anyone . . . save one, who is the master of all." There was no middle ground "between the sovereignty of all and the absolute power of one man." In his astonishing prediction of 20th-century totalitarian dictatorship, Tocqueville explained how the revolution of equality could lead to the "*Führerprinzip*" and more terrible absolutism than the world had ever known.

But when rights are given to every citizen and the sovereignty of all is established, the problem of leadership takes a new form, becomes more exacting than ever before. It is easy to issue commands and enforce them by the rope and the stake, the concentration camp and the *gulag*. It is much harder to use argument and achievement to overcome opposition and win consent. The Founding Fathers of the United States understood the difficulty. They believed that history had given them the opportunity to decide, as Alexander Hamilton wrote in the first Federalist Paper, whether men are indeed capable of basing government on "reflection and choice, or whether they are forever destined to depend . . . on accident and force."

Government by reflection and choice called for a new style of leadership and a new quality of followership. It required leaders to be responsive to popular concerns, and it required followers to be active and informed participants in the process. Democracy does not eliminate emotion from politics; sometimes it fosters demagoguery; but it is confident that, as the greatest of democratic leaders put it, you cannot fool all of the people all of the time. It measures leadership by results and retires those who overreach or falter or fail.

It is true that in the long run despots are measured by results too. But they can postpone the day of judgment, sometimes indefinitely, and in the meantime they can do infinite harm. It is also true that democracy is no guarantee of virtue and intelligence in government, for the voice of the people is not necessarily the voice of God. But democracy, by assuring the right of opposition, offers built-in resistance to the evils inherent in absolutism. As the theologian Reinhold Niebuhr summed it up, "Man's capacity for justice makes democracy possible, but man's inclination to injustice makes democracy necessary."

A second test for leadership is the end for which power is sought. When leaders have as their goal the supremacy of a master race or the promotion of totalitarian revolution or the acquisition and exploitation of colonies or the protection of greed and privilege or the preservation of personal power, it is likely that their leadership will do little to advance the cause of humanity. When their goal is the abolition of slavery, the liberation of women, the enlargement of opportunity for the poor and powerless, the extension of equal rights to racial minorities, the defense of the freedoms of expression and opposition, it is likely that their leadership will increase the sum of human liberty and welfare.

Leaders have done great harm to the world. They have also conferred great benefits. You will find both sorts in this series. Even "good" leaders must be regarded with a certain wariness. Leaders are not demigods; they put on their trousers one leg after another just like ordinary mortals. No leader is infallible, and every leader needs to be reminded of this at regular intervals. Irreverence irritates leaders but is their salvation. Unquestioning submission corrupts leaders and demeans followers. Making a cult of a leader is always a mistake. Fortunately hero worship generates its own antidote. "Every hero," said Emerson, "becomes a bore at last."

The signal benefit the great leaders confer is to embolden the rest of us to live according to our own best selves, to be active, insistent, and resolute in affirming our own sense of things. For great leaders attest to the reality of human freedom against the supposed inevitabilities of history. And they attest to the wisdom and power that may lie within the most unlikely of us, which is why Abraham Lincoln remains the supreme example of great leadership. A great leader, said Emerson, exhibits new possibilities to all humanity. "We feed on genius. . . . Great men exist that there may be greater men."

Great leaders, in short, justify themselves by emancipating and empowering their followers. So humanity struggles to master its destiny, remembering with Alexis de Tocqueville: "It is true that around every man a fatal circle is traced beyond which he cannot pass; but within the wide verge of that circle he is powerful and free; as it is with man, so with communities."

1

Hanging Together

Never contradict anybody.
—BENJAMIN FRANKLIN
to Thomas Jefferson

Philadelphia, Pennsylvania, Monday, September 17, 1787. Benjamin Franklin made his way to the Pennsylvania State House (now called Independence Hall), as he had been doing nearly every day for four months while the federal convention met to form a new plan of government. The delegates had finally hammered out a Constitution and had arranged for it to be transcribed onto parchment over the weekend so that it could be signed on Monday. Franklin, at 81, was the oldest delegate to the convention, and on that morning he was to give a speech — certainly the most important one of his life — with which he hoped to persuade the other delegates to approve the Constitution unanimously.

Franklin could well remember the day 11 years earlier—July 4, 1776—when he had signed the Declaration of Independence in the same place. The patriots had taken a bold risk, rebelling against the vastly superior strength of Great Britain, and Franklin is said to have remarked wryly to the other signers, "Gentlemen, we must now all hang together, or we shall most assuredly hang separately." Now, in 1787, having won in a bloody war the political freedom they had declared in 1776, Franklin

When Benjamin Franklin left his hometown of Boston in 1723, at the age of 17, he did so with high expectations; colonial America, he believed, was a land of unbounded opportunity. By the time of his death in 1790, Citizen Franklin had become the embodiment of American success.

Members of the Continental Congress look on as Benjamin Franklin signs the Declaration of Independence on July 2, 1776, in Philadelphia. Franklin, at 70, was the oldest of the 56 men who signed the document.

and his fellow Constitutional Convention delegates were taking a different kind of risk, and the outcome of their efforts was again uncertain.

They were proposing to unite the 13 states under a more powerful central government. Many citizens — perhaps most — did not want a stronger federal government. They had just thrown off the authority of the British crown and were not eager to be dominated again. Still, many were convinced that the United States needed a more vigorous central authority in order to survive. In the interest of convincing the delegates once again to "hang together," Franklin prepared his speech.

The weekend had been rainy, but that morning it was clear and cool. Suffering from gout, gallstones, and other infirmities of old age, Franklin had found the convention an exhausting experience. When he was feeling well enough, he walked the few blocks from his house. But sometimes he felt weak, or the weather was bad, and on these occasions he was carried to the East Room of the State House in a specially constructed sedan chair. The sight of the rotund Franklin, suspended in his glassed-in box between two flexible poles that

swayed gently as four convicts from the Walnut Street jail bore their distinguished cargo, was a familiar one to his neighbors.

The convention had been meeting throughout the hot summer and disputes over the details of the new form of government had been intense. During Franklin's long career in public service, he had always taken on the diplomatic tasks, calming tempers and mending differences. This had also been his role in the convention, and he hoped his speech that morning would have a conciliatory effect.

Never a great public speaker, Franklin had participated little in the formal proceedings of the convention. He preferred to exert his influence behind the scenes and often entertained fellow delegates at his home in order to do so. On one such occasion, a visitor to the city came to Franklin's house and found him seated — "a short, fat, trunched old man in plain Quaker dress, bald pate, and short white locks" — in his garden under a mulberry tree with a group of men and women. In the course of the conversation, Franklin showed his guests a curiosity he had just received — a two-headed snake preserved in a jar. Franklin wondered aloud what would happen if the snake, traveling along the ground, came to the stem of a bush, and one of its heads chose to go on one side of the stem while the other preferred to pass on the opposite side. If neither head would compromise and come back to pass on the same side as the other head, the poor snake would be stuck.

No doubt the guests knew that this story had a point; Franklin had used the snake as a symbol for America several times before. In 1751, when Great Britain was sending criminals to its American colonies, Franklin wrote that the colonies should retaliate by exporting "the venomous reptiles we call rattle-snakes" to London. In 1754, he drew a cartoon (the first political cartoon to be published in America), and printed it in his newspaper, the *Pennsylvania Gazette*, depicting the colonies as a snake divided into eight pieces, with the words "Join, or Die" below. The frontier was then being threatened by the French and Indians, and Franklin believed that stronger colonial unity was necessary

Observed by curious Indians and welcomed by fascinated ladies, an ailing Ben Franklin arrives at the Pennsylvania State House in a special carriage borne by convicts.

to defend the English settlements. In 1775, at the start of the Revolution, the rattlesnake was adopted as a military emblem, and the accompanying caption, "Don't tread on me," was an unmistakable warning to the British. The two-headed snake in the anecdote Franklin told in his garden was a new variation, but its meaning was clear to Franklin's listeners: American unity was still necessary if the Constitution was to succeed, and political compromise was essential if that unity was to be achieved.

After General George Washington, the president of the convention, called the session to order and had the Constitution read aloud, Franklin's prestige entitled him to speak first. Because he could not stand on his feet for long, he had his fellow Pennsylvanian, James Wilson, read the speech for him.

Franklin began the address by admitting that he was not entirely happy with all parts of the Constitution. But he added that he had often found it wise to doubt his own judgment and to listen to the reasoning of others, rather than to insist stubbornly on the correctness of his own views. To emphasize this point, an anecdote about a French lady who had a disagreement with her sister was offered. "I don't know how it happens, Sister," the lady said, "but I meet with no body but my self that's always in the right."

When the laughter of the delegates died down, Wilson continued reading Franklin's speech: "I agree to this Constitution with all its faults, if they are such . . . I doubt too whether any other Convention we can obtain may be able to make a better Constitution. For when you assemble a number of men to have the advantage of their joint wisdom, you inevitably assemble with those men, all their prejudices, their passions, their errors of opinion, their local interests, and their selfish views. From such an Assembly can a perfect production be expected?"

Given the imperfection of ordinary men, Franklin believed, the Constitution was as near perfection as could be hoped for, and the advantages its ratification would secure were much greater than the

Thus I consent . . . to this Constitution, because I expect no better, and because I am not sure that it is not the best.

—BENJAMIN FRANKLIN

disadvantages that would result from its rejection. "On the whole," Franklin concluded, "I cannot help expressing a wish that every member of the Convention who may still have objections to it, would with me, on this occasion doubt a little of his own infallibility — and to make manifest our unanimity, put his name to this instrument."

The speech did not convince everyone, but ultimately only two delegates resisted Franklin's persuasive power and refused to sign. While the members of the convention were authorizing the document, Franklin looked at the chair from which George Washington had been presiding over the convention. On the back of the chair a picture of the sun was painted. Contemplating the painting, Franklin said that he had never been sure whether the painter had meant it to be a rising sun or a setting sun. "But now," he continued, "I have the happiness to know that it is a rising and not a setting Sun."

Benjamin Franklin was born in Puritan Boston on January 17, 1706. His family was large: He was the 15th child born to his father, Josiah Franklin. Three of those children had died before Benjamin's birth, and of the surviving 11, 6 were brothers and 5 were sisters. Benjamin would be the final son born in the family, but two more sisters would follow him. His mother, Abiah Folger Franklin, a redoubtable homemaker, was his father's second wife (his first wife had died after giving birth to her seventh child), and Benjamin was her eighth child.

Josiah Franklin had been born in the small village in England where his family had lived for centuries. He was an intelligent, articulate, and industrious man. His trade had been that of a dyer of textiles. When Josiah, his first wife, Anne, and their first 3 children arrived in America in 1683, he found that in the simpler society of Boston (with only about 5,000 inhabitants) there was little demand for dyed cloth. He therefore took up the trade of a soap and candle maker. In 1703, they suffered a misfortune when one of the children, Ebenezer, drowned in a tub of suds at the age of 16 months. The Franklin

Franklin, who preferred to exercise his political influence within a social setting, entertains guests in the garden of his Philadelphia home. One of his grandchildren is at his side, and his daughter Sally is pouring tea for Alexander Hamilton.

shop and home were together on Milk Street, opposite the Old South Church, where the family attended services regularly.

By the time his father's older brother Benjamin, a widower, came from England in 1715 and joined the household, most of young Benjamin's brothers and sisters had married and moved out. Uncle Benjamin took a special interest in his namesake, writing poems for him that contained moral advice and teaching him shorthand. This skill, he hoped, would be of use in recording sermons if Franklin became a minister, as his father for a time intended.

Young Benjamin liked to read books and was bright and inquisitive, and so at the age of eight his father sent him to a local school, meaning eventually to educate him at Harvard to be a clergyman. (All of his older brothers had been apprenticed to various tradesmen.) Benjamin learned to write easily but failed in arithmetic. At 10 years of age, he was taken out of school and put to work at home as his father's assistant.

He cut wicks for the candles, filled the molds, waited on customers in the shop, and went on various errands. But he soon found that he disliked his father's trade, and he began to dream of becoming a sailor like his older brother Josiah, who had run off to sea. Benjamin would often spend his free time in and around the water, swimming and fishing with his friends, and sometimes making mischief.

Undaunted by the bitter New England winter, a devout family of Bostonians comes out of church. Franklin was raised in a Puritan family, but he never fully embraced the austere Puritan ethic.

On one occasion, he convinced some other boys to join him in building a wharf in a pond where they fished for minnows, so that they would not have to stand in the mud. They stole large stones in the evening from a nearby site where a house was being built and constructed their wharf, but the workmen returned in the morning to find the stones missing and found both the wharf and the culprits who had built it. The fledgling engineer was "corrected" by his father, in spite of his argument that the wharf was a useful project. Josiah explained that "nothing was useful which was not honest."

When he saw that Benjamin was unhappy about following in his trade, Josiah began to look around for something more to his son's liking. Together they visited many different tradesmen, but Benjamin could not find a business that he would be satisfied with. Finally, considering Benjamin's talent for reading, it was arranged for him to be the apprentice of his older brother James, then 21, who had just returned from England with a printing press and materials to set himself up as a printer. Benjamin was reluctant but eventually agreed; and in 1718, at the age of 12, he signed his indentures — the legal contract that committed him to work for his brother until he was 21, providing his labor in exchange for the training he would receive and the food, clothing, and shelter his brother would provide. This was the usual way in which an ordinary family would help its members get started in life. Benjamin soon became a skillful worker in his brother's shop. More important, however, the printer's trade opened up a new world to him — the world of literature and ideas.

Although Puritan Boston was not as somber a place as it is sometimes represented to have been, the people were serious and devout. In the early years of the 18th century, however, the power of the Puritan ministers was beginning to decline, and new cultural influences were gaining ground. Benjamin's brother James used his printing shop to promote these radical trends. In the company of James and his like-minded friends, Benjamin

Young Ben Franklin hard at work as an apprentice in his brother James's printing shop. It was during his apprenticeship to his brother that Franklin developed his love for the printed word.

learned to be less pious than his parents and the local ministers might have liked. He already had a healthy streak of irreverence in him, as he had demonstrated once in his father's house. Benjamin, who had a healthy appetite even as a boy, often grew impatient and hungry while his father prayed before meals. One day, when the food they were preserving and storing for the winter had been sealed in a large cask, Benjamin suggested that all of it be blessed at once, so as to save the time it took to do so at every meal.

Benjamin came into contact with the apprentices of booksellers with whom James did business, and he would often "borrow" books from them in the evening, read them all night, and return them in the morning before they were missed, taking care not to smear them with his ink-stained hands. A friend of his brother's, Matthew Adams, who owned a decent library, began to allow Benjamin to borrow whatever he liked. Taking an interest in poetry, Benjamin then wrote some himself, using recent events as his subjects. A ballad he wrote on the drowning of a lighthouse keeper and his two daughters was immediately printed in the shop, and Benjamin took the sheets around in the streets to sell them, pleased at finding that they were popular. At the age of 13, Benjamin Franklin's literary career had begun.

One of James Franklin's contracts was for printing the *Boston Gazette*. After 10 months, the contract was given to another printer, and James responded by launching his own newspaper. In August 1721, the first issue of the *New England Courant* came off his press, and Benjamin, after composing the type and printing the pages, took to the streets to distribute the new publication. James and his friends made it a success by including in it humorous and satirical essays in addition to the ordinary news. Some of their daring satires were directed against Cotton Mather and other Puritan leaders, however, and in the next few years James was imprisoned twice for having offended those in power. During his imprisonment, Benjamin carried on the publishing, and he was bold enough "to give our Rulers some Rubs in it."

Benjamin slowly began to resent the authority his brother exercised over him. The example of the clever men who wrote for the *Courant* had inspired Benjamin with the ambition to be a writer himself, but he felt certain his brother would be unwilling to publish anything he wrote. He therefore outwitted James by writing his essays in secret and slipping them under the door of the printing house at night. He signed them "Silence Dogood," and no one suspected that he, a 16-year-old boy, was the author of such delightfully witty writings.

He kept silent while James and his friends admired the essays, tried to guess the author, and gladly printed them in the newspaper. Benjamin continued to write under the same name until he had written 14 in all. When he finally revealed that he was Silence Dogood, the wits who wrote for the *Courant* began to treat him with more respect than they had when he was known to them as a mere printer's apprentice. James, however, resented his younger brother's achievement, and Benjamin, in turn, was even less willing to accept James's authority. They quarreled frequently and sometimes

The Bent of his mind was . . . unmistakable. . . . For the lad who could deny himself the few treats afforded by a Puritan town, save his coppers and lay them out on such books as were then to be had at Boston, there seemed to be but one career, the career of a man of letters.

—JOHN BACH MCMASTER
Franklin biographer

came to blows. The brothers could not continue to be master and apprentice for long, and Benjamin began to look for an opportunity to escape his unhappy situation.

On Wednesday, September 25, 1723, Benjamin, with his close friend John Collins, boarded a ship in the middle of the night. After three days of swift sailing the ship arrived at New York, where Benjamin sought work in a printing shop owned by William Bradford. Business was slow, however, and Bradford could not hire him; but he thought that his son, a printer in Philadelphia whose most valued assistant had just died, might need a new employee. Once again, 17-year-old Benjamin Franklin, already 300 miles from home, with little money in his pocket, set out for an unfamiliar destination.

On Tuesday, October 1, he departed in a small boat for New Jersey, but a storm pushed the boat back toward Long Island. Unable to go ashore because of the choppy water, he and his fellow passengers spent the night huddled in the boat, wet to the skin by the waves that crashed over them. When the wind died down the next day, they got to New

Franklin, a teenage man of letters, hawks his first literary effort on the streets of Boston at the age of 13. The verses sold well and thus launched Franklin's successful literary career.

A sailor imparts a few words of advice to a young man intent on seeking his fortune at sea. Stifled by his brother's disapproval and by staid Puritan Boston, Franklin soon embarked on his own maritime venture.

Jersey, where Franklin spent the night in an inn, sweating feverishly. The next day he began the 50-mile walk to Burlington, New Jersey, where he understood he would find a boat to sail the rest of the way to Philadelphia. Tired and hungry, he walked until noon in the rain and then took refuge in another inn; the next day he continued his trek, by evening reaching an inn within a few miles of Burlington. When he finally got to the town the next morning, Saturday, October 5, he learned that there would not be a boat to Philadelphia until Tuesday; he therefore found a lodging house in which to wait, but while walking along the river that evening a boat came along that was going to Philadelphia, and he was offered a place on it. There was no wind to propel them, so they rowed until midnight, anchored the boat in a creek, made a fire, and slept until daybreak in the cold autumn air. In the morning they found that they were only a little above Philadelphia, and by eight or nine o'clock they had rowed the rest of the way. They landed at the Market Street Wharf, where Franklin, bedraggled, broke, and uncertain of the future, disembarked and entered the city of Philadelphia.

2

A Rational Creature

Diligence is the Mother of good luck.
—*Poor Richard's Almanack*

In 1723, Philadelphia was a relatively new town (founded in 1681), with fewer than 10,000 inhabitants. It was not the equal of Boston in trade or culture, but within the next 50 years it would grow rapidly and surpass Boston to become the most important city in the American colonies and the second largest city — next to London — in the British Empire. Benjamin Franklin had come to the right place at the right time, and his future success would coincide with that of his adopted city.

Philadelphia was strikingly different from Boston in its social structure and style of life. Founded by William Penn, a Quaker, the city's character was defined by the tolerance of diversity that the Quakers exemplified. There was no official church, as there was in Massachusetts, and no class of ministers who dictated social norms. People practiced their different faiths as they pleased. Philadelphia was also the main point of entry for the immigrants (mostly Germans and so-called Scotch-Irish from the north of Ireland) who were beginning to swell Pennsylvania's population. Thus ethnic as well as religious diversity characterized Philadelphia, and in this respect it was a city of the future, prefiguring social developments in the rest of America.

These conditions were agreeable to the young Benjamin Franklin, whose free-ranging mind had

Upon arriving in colonial Philadelphia in 1723, a hungry Benjamin Franklin spent his last three cents on three loaves of bread. "Having no room in my pockets," Franklin later recalled, "I walk'd off with a roll under each arm, and eating the other."

been stifled in conservative Boston. His immediate concern, however, was to find a job and a place to live and to begin to make his way in this new environment. On his second day in Philadelphia he found a position as a journeyman printer in the shop of Samuel Keimer, who had only just set up as the second printer in town. (Andrew Bradford, the other printer and son of the New York printer William Bradford, had been unable to offer Benjamin any work.) Benjamin found a room in a boardinghouse next door to Keimer's shop. His landlord was John Read, whose daughter Deborah would later become Franklin's wife.

While working hard in Keimer's shop and getting to know Deborah, Benjamin began to make friends among the literate young men of the city. He even got to know the governor, Sir William Keith, by a quirk of fate. Benjamin's brother-in-law, Robert Holmes, a ship's captain, wrote to young Ben on behalf of the family in Boston, urging him to come home and assuring him of his family's forgiveness. Benjamin wrote back, explaining his reasons for leaving home and describing his plans for his life in Philadelphia, and Holmes happened to show this letter to Governor Keith, who was an acquaintance of his. The governor was impressed by the intelligence, maturity, and ambition the letter displayed, and he soon came to look for this promising young man in Keimer's shop. Keimer naturally assumed the unexpected visit was to him as the proprietor of the shop, but Keith sought out the 18-year-old employee and invited him to a nearby tavern for a glass of wine. Keimer was quite taken aback to see the governor of Pennsylvania showing such interest in this unknown young worker; Benjamin later wrote in his autobiography, "I was not a little surpriz'd, and Keimer star'd like a Pig poison'd."

God gives all things to industry. He that hath a trade hath an estate.

—Poor Richard's Almanack

At the tavern, Governor Keith made a proposal. The two printers in town — Bradford and Keimer — were poorly qualified and did miserable work. If Benjamin were to start his own printing business, the governor would give him plenty of work printing official documents. Benjamin was flattered but had no money with which to start a business, and he

William Penn (standing with outstretched arms), founder and proprietor of the province of Pennsylvania, negotiates a treaty with local Indians in 1681. Penn, a Quaker, encouraged people of all religions to settle in his province.

doubted that his father would assist him financially. Governor Keith therefore wrote a letter to Josiah Franklin, urging him to help his son, and with this letter in hand Benjamin returned to Boston. Even a letter from the governor of Pennsylvania did not sway Josiah, however; he thought Benjamin was too young to undertake such a venture. Benjamin returned to Philadelphia with plenty of fatherly advice but no money.

Governor Keith now promised to provide Benjamin with the funds to establish his enterprise, and he recommended that Benjamin travel to London to obtain the necessary equipment and to establish the right business connections. While waiting for a ship to take him to England, where he would purchase a press, types, and other materials, Benjamin continued to work for Keimer, saying nothing of his plan to set up as a competitor. He continued his courtship of Deborah Read as well, but her mother urged them not to marry until Benjamin returned from London. In the meantime, he joined with his friends in reading and writing, critiquing one another's compositions, and trying to improve their language skills. In colonial Philadelphia, the acquisition of such skills was extremely important, just as it is today, so Benjamin and his friends worked

The sun sets behind the Tower of London. Benjamin Franklin arrived in the British capital for the first time on Christmas Eve, 1724; he fell in love with the city immediately.

diligently, aspiring to climb the social ladder. Governor Keith regularly invited Benjamin to dinner at his house and always spoke of the plan to open a new printing office as a definite thing.

When it came time to sail for England, Benjamin exchanged promises with Deborah Read and went aboard with his friend James Ralph, a merchant's clerk who hoped to begin a literary career in London (and who was abandoning his wife and young child in Philadelphia). Governor Keith had promised to put letters on board, directed to businessmen in London who would extend credit to Benjamin, which would enable him to obtain the equipment for his printing shop. Franklin mistakenly assumed the letters had been put into the ship's mail sack, and only when he reached England did he discover that Governor Keith had sent no letters at all. A merchant who had taken an interest in Benjamin during passage, Thomas Denham, explained that Governor Keith was known to be an untrustworthy character and a man who made promises he could not keep. Denham urged Benjamin to make the best of the situation by getting work with a printer in London to gain experience that would be useful once he returned to America.

Franklin enjoyed London immensely. Finding work at Samuel Palmer's printing office and lodging with Ralph — who did not find work so quickly and therefore lived off of his friend's earnings — Franklin went to the theater, enjoyed himself in taverns, consorted with prostitutes and intellectuals, and soon forgot the fiancée he had left behind. He continued his literary self-education by borrowing books from the bookseller John Wilcox, who lived next door. At Palmer's printing shop, one of the books for which he composed the type was a religious tract by William Wollaston called *The Religion of Nature Delineated*. Finding that he disagreed with Wollaston's reasoning, Benjamin wrote a rejoinder, in which he argued that there was no such thing as free will — that everything happened in the world as it was fated to happen and that there was consequently no reason for men to try to act virtuously. Printing up several copies himself, he called his pamphlet *A Dissertation on Liberty and Necessity, Pleasure and Pain*. It was an impressive performance for a 19-year-old, although Franklin would later reject its principles as dangerous; nevertheless, it brought him to the attention of some of the leading intellectuals of London and his employer, Palmer, held him in higher esteem.

Benjamin saved money as well as he could, anticipating his return home. He also made money by charging interest on the loans he made to fellow workmen when they were short of cash and wanted to buy beer. Ralph moved out of the quarters he shared with Franklin, who was then able to move to cheaper lodgings. At one point, after teaching several friends to swim in the Thames River and impressing others with his own swimming abilities, Franklin considered traveling around Europe and supporting himself by offering swimming lessons. But Denham, his merchant friend, dissuaded Franklin by hiring him as a clerk for his business in Philadelphia. Thus after a pleasant year and a half in London, Benjamin sailed for Philadelphia.

While on board ship this time he kept a journal of the voyage, in which he recorded his thoughts and observations. Once, when a man was caught cheating at cards, an informal court of law was assembled and the man was found guilty and ordered to pay a fine. He refused and was therefore, Franklin said, "excommunicated" from shipboard society. After five days during which no one would speak with him, he relented and paid his fine. Franklin observed that "we have this morning received him into unity again. Man is a sociable being, and it is for aught I know one of the worst punishments to be excluded from society." These reflections were certainly true of Franklin himself; he was a social being by nature and the limited society of the ship was inadequate to his need for human contact. When a sail was sighted one day, the captain slowed down to allow the other ship to catch up. Franklin reflected that "there is really something strangely cheering to the spirits in the meeting of a ship at sea, containing a society of creatures of the same species and in the same circumstances with ourselves, after we had been long separated and excommunicated as it were from the rest of mankind. My

Franklin (seated at left), is toasted by fellow workers at Palmer's printing shop in London. Benjamin frequently lent them money to buy beer, but he always charged a healthy interest rate on the loans.

Patrons of a London tavern enjoy a quiet afternoon of pipe smoking, ale, and conversation. The cozy taverns and boisterous pubs of London were among Franklin's favorite haunts.

heart fluttered in my breast with joy when I saw so many human countenances, and I could scarce refrain from that kind of laughter which proceeds from some degree of inward pleasure."

In his maritime journal, Benjamin also recorded changes in the weather, and on a day when the wind rose and there was "the most violent shower of rain I ever saw," the foamy white surface of the water led Franklin to record that "the sea looked like a cream dish." He also recorded what he called a "Plan of Conduct," in which he reviewed his life and stated his intentions for the future: "I have never fixed a regular design in life; by which means it has been a confused variety of different scenes. I am now entering upon a new one: let me, therefore, make some resolutions, and form some scheme of action, that, henceforth, I may live in all respects like a rational

After 18 months in England, Franklin sailed for Philadelphia. The eight-week voyage provided an ideal setting for contemplation, and by the time he arrived in America, Franklin had formulated the "rational" philosophy by which he was to live the rest of his life.

creature." This intention — to conduct his life according to rational principles — was thoroughly characteristic of Franklin, and he would make similar resolutions periodically throughout his life.

Back in Philadelphia, Denham fell ill early in 1727, and Benjamin had to find new work once again. He was sick himself, however, in March and

April of 1727, with pleurisy (inflammation of the membrane surrounding the lungs). "I suffered a good deal . . . & was rather disappointed when I found myself recovering; regretting in some degree that I must sometime or other have all that disagreeable Work to do over again." He would live to the age of 84 and so would not have to endure such an experience again for a long time, but this admission of despair is an unusual one for the ordinarily calm and cheerful Franklin, and it gives a rare hint of the darker emotions that his carefully crafted rational personality usually disguised.

Denham died late in 1727, and by that time Franklin, recovered from his illness, had been back at work in Keimer's shop for a year. Franklin's superb skills as a printer led Keimer to put him in charge of the other printers in the office and pay him well for his talents, but when the other workers improved under Franklin's supervision, Keimer wanted Franklin to accept a cut in pay. The two of them quarreled and Franklin abruptly quit.

With one of the other young men in Keimer's shop, Hugh Meredith, Franklin opened his own business; Meredith's father loaned them the money. They planned to publish a newspaper, but when the disgruntled Keimer heard of this, he rushed into print with his own paper, calling it the *Pennsylvania Gazette* and hoping to attract subscribers first and thereby to get a jump on Franklin. Franklin got even with Keimer by putting his literary talents to use: He wrote a series of humorous essays for the *American Weekly Mercury*, a rival paper published by Andrew Bradford, and the essays (published under the pen name "The Busy Body") diverted readership from Keimer's new paper. The *Pennsylvania Gazette* began to fail, and in September 1729, Franklin bought it from Keimer. He was finally able to put his skills as a writer to use for his own purposes, and the intelligence and humor of the *Gazette* under Franklin's editorship made it the most widely read newspaper in the American colonies. Benjamin Franklin was on his way, and he was soon to be one of the most successful and influential men in America.

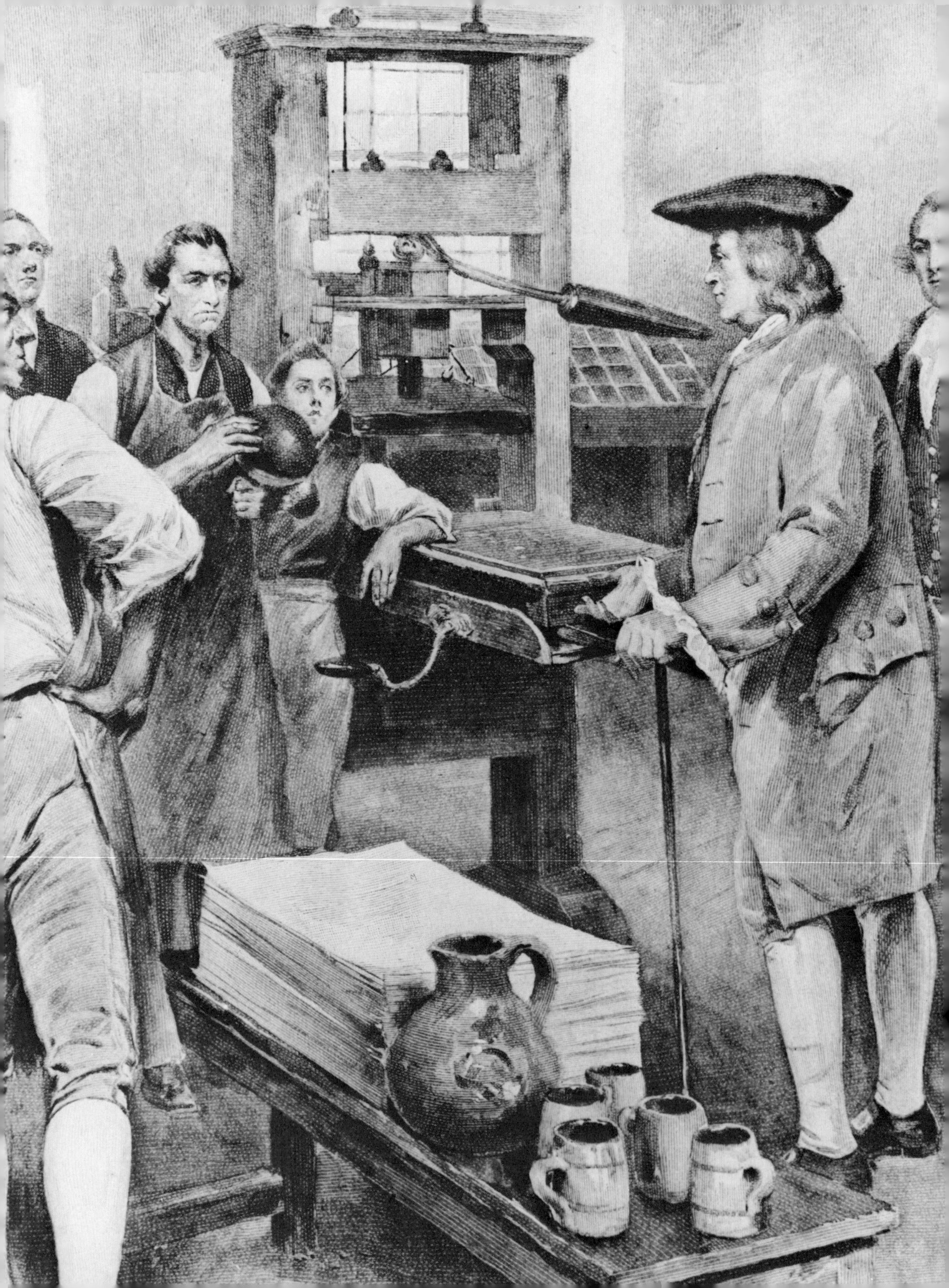

3
Poor Richard

> ***What you would seem to be, be really.***
> —*Poor Richard's Almanack*

By 1730, with success on the horizon, Franklin had come to certain decisions about his personal life and the principles by which he would try to live. He came to regret *Pleasure and Pain*, the religious pamphlet he had published in London, because although he believed it made sense as a logical argument, he feared that its principles led only to unethical and irresponsible behavior. In the pamphlet he had argued that man had no free will and therefore need not worry about the difference between good actions and bad — he could do nothing to change the course of events. Such "freethinking," Franklin came to believe, had led him into moral carelessness of various kinds and had led him to encourage such carelessness in others. He admitted, for example, that he visited prostitutes. In his autobiography he referred to such moral infractions as *errata*, a printer's term meaning misprint.

Among the actions he regretted most was his abandonment of Deborah Read when he went to London. During his absence, Deborah had felt lonely and neglected, and she had finally given up on Benjamin and married someone else. This man deserted her after only a few months and was never heard from again. In 1730, Franklin fathered a child

Benjamin Franklin (wearing a three-cornered hat) instructs the workers at his Philadelphia printing shop. His purchase of the *Pennsylvania Gazette* marked the beginning of his career as a publisher and editor, and with the appearance of *Poor Richard's Almanack* in 1731, Franklin became the most popular writer in the colonies.

Franklin took Deborah Read of Philadelphia as his common-law wife in 1730. "She proved," Franklin said of her later, "a good and faithful helpmate . . . we throve together . . . and have ever mutually endeavour'd to make each other happy."

by an unknown woman, a boy named William — one of his most serious errata during this time of his life. Wishing to settle down and leave his youthful missteps behind, Franklin sought to marry a young female relative of the family with which he then boarded, but he asked for a dowry, a quantity of money or property that a girl's family often gave as a gift to the young man she married. Her family refused. Franklin lost interest in the girl and began to show a new interest in Deborah Read (now Deborah Rogers). However, because her legal husband was gone but not known to be dead, Deborah was not free to marry again; and if Franklin married her, he feared he might be held accountable for the debts her first husband left behind. So Benjamin and Deborah resolved to live together in what was called a common-law union (without legal sanction), but in every respect as husband and wife, and they took Benjamin's illegitimate son, William, into their home. This arrangement was not, at that time, socially unacceptable.

Deborah proved to be a valued mate. She worked in Franklin's shop and ran their household as well. She was not an educated woman and other people reported that she was sometimes loud and uncouth and had an unruly temper, but she was completely devoted to her husband's interests. She was a strong, healthy, plump woman, and Franklin once wrote to her that a beer jug he bought and sent as a gift "looked like a fat, jolly Dame, clean and tidy, with a neat blue and white Calico Gown on, good-natured and lovely" and reminded him strongly of her. Deborah bore two children, a boy named Francis on October 20, 1732 (who died of smallpox four years later), and a girl named Sarah on August 31, 1743 (called Sally, she lived to adulthood). Franklin had wanted a large family, and at that time women usually bore many children, but these were to be Franklin's only offspring with Deborah.

> ***He that hath not got a Wife, is not yet a Compleat Man.***
> *—Poor Richard's Almanack*

In the early years of his married life, Franklin engaged in many constructive social projects, along with his efforts to secure his own livelihood. In 1730, he was named official printer of Pennsylvania, and he thereafter printed the colony's currency and documents. In 1731, he formed the first public library in the American colonies. It was a subscription library; people pooled their money to buy a collection of books from which they could then borrow. Also in 1731, Franklin established one of his employees, Thomas Whitmarsh, as a printer in South Carolina; Franklin provided the equipment and materials and then shared in the profits. This was the first of several such sponsorships and proved to be a good investment for Franklin. He would later sponsor other apprentices in setting up printing shops, in New York; Antigua, the West Indies; and Lancaster, Pennsylvania.

Franklin founded a German-language newspaper in 1731, seeing a market for such a publication among the many immigrants who were coming to Pennsylvania at that time. It soon failed, but during the same year he began publishing what would become a very successful and influential annual work, *Poor Richard's Almanack*. All the printers published almanacs, which featured a calendar that showed the phases of the moon, predicted the weather and tides, and gave other pertinent meteorologic and agricultural information. The almanacs also offered bits of homespun advice, colloquial humor, regional recipes, and other odds and ends of folk wisdom and information. Franklin's almanac was packed with the proverbs that came to shape and define American culture: "A penny saved is a penny earned," and so forth. Most of these sayings were not made up by Franklin himself but borrowed from various books that he had acquired. He usually adapted and rewrote them, however, simplifying and modifying their phrasing to make them fit American circumstances. Among the well-known sayings from *Poor Richard's Almanack* were these: "No gains without pains"; "Early to bed and early to rise, makes a man healthy, wealthy, and wise"; "God helps them that help themselves"; "Haste makes waste"; and "One half of the world does not know how the other half lives."

Poor Richard's Almanack was an unprecedented success; in the colonies, only the Bible sold more. The proverbs and maxims in *Poor Richard's* were endlessly quoted and repeated over the years, until they became the "common sense" of millions of

Franklin put his love for books to practical use in 1731, when he established the first public library in the colonies. By 1741, the subscription library's catalogue listed 375 titles, most of them in history and literature.

Americans. Most of the maxims focused on what would come to be the American work ethic, which essentially promised that hard work, clean living, and perseverance would bring success. Franklin must be credited, therefore, with forming and shaping a large part of the characteristic outlook and values of a burgeoning popular culture. He was America's first pop philosopher and moralist, the precursor to such men as Mark Twain and Horatio Alger.

In his autobiography, Franklin tells how, in 1733, he conceived "the bold and arduous Project of arriving at moral Perfection." His sarcastic description of this project indicates that he did not take it quite as solemnly as one might think. But evidently he did devise a method of moral improvement that he followed with some determination at the time. This method consisted of forming a set of resolutions concerning the moral virtues he wished to develop. There were 12 in all: Temperance, Silence, Order, Resolution, Frugality, Industry, Sincerity, Justice, Moderation, Cleanliness, Tranquillity, and Chastity. A Quaker friend advised him that people considered him somewhat arrogant, so Franklin wryly added a 13th virtue, Humility, to the list.

Franklin then set about to make the practice of these virtues habitual. He designed a chart on which he would record every failure to practice one or another of the virtues. The chart had 7 columns, 1 for each day of the week, and 13 lines, 1 for each of the 13 virtues. Because he felt it would be too difficult to attack all his faults at once, he devoted a week to each virtue; and whenever he failed, he made a "little black Spot" on the appropriate line and in the proper column on the chart. Thus he could go through the 13 virtues in as many weeks, and go through the entire process 4 times during the 52 weeks of a year. The cleaner he kept the chart, the more virtuous he could believe he was becoming. Eventually, Franklin transferred the chart, which he had drawn on paper, to an ivory tablet; it would be more durable, and he could rub out the black marks at the end of the 13 weeks without tearing holes in the chart. As he grew older, he put himself

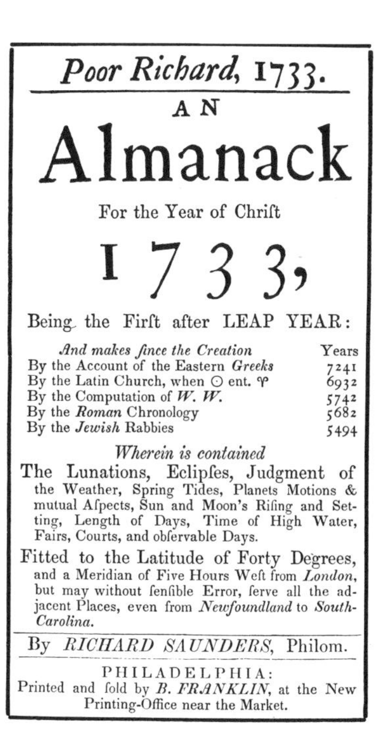

Poor Richard, 1733.

AN

Almanack

For the Year of Chrift

1733,

Being the Firft after LEAP YEAR:

And makes fince the Creation	Years
By the Account of the Eastern *Greeks*	7241
By the Latin Church, when ☉ ent. ♈	6932
By the Computation of *W. W.*	5742
By the *Roman* Chronology	5682
By the *Jewish* Rabbies	5494

Wherein is contained

The Lunations, Eclipfes, Judgment of the Weather, Spring Tides, Planets Motions & mutual Afpects, Sun and Moon's Rifing and Setting, Length of Days, Time of High Water, Fairs, Courts, and obfervable Days.

Fitted to the Latitude of Forty Degrees, and a Meridian of Five Hours Weft from *London,* but may without fenfible Error, ferve all the adjacent Places, even from *Newfoundland* to *South-Carolina.*

By *RICHARD SAUNDERS,* Philom.

PHILADELPHIA:
Printed and fold by *B. FRANKLIN,* at the New Printing-Office near the Market.

The 1733 issue of *Poor Richard's Almanack*, "printed and sold by B. Franklin." *Poor Richard's* served as a manual for everyday living in mid-18th-century America, and a copy of the latest issue could be found in most colonial kitchens.

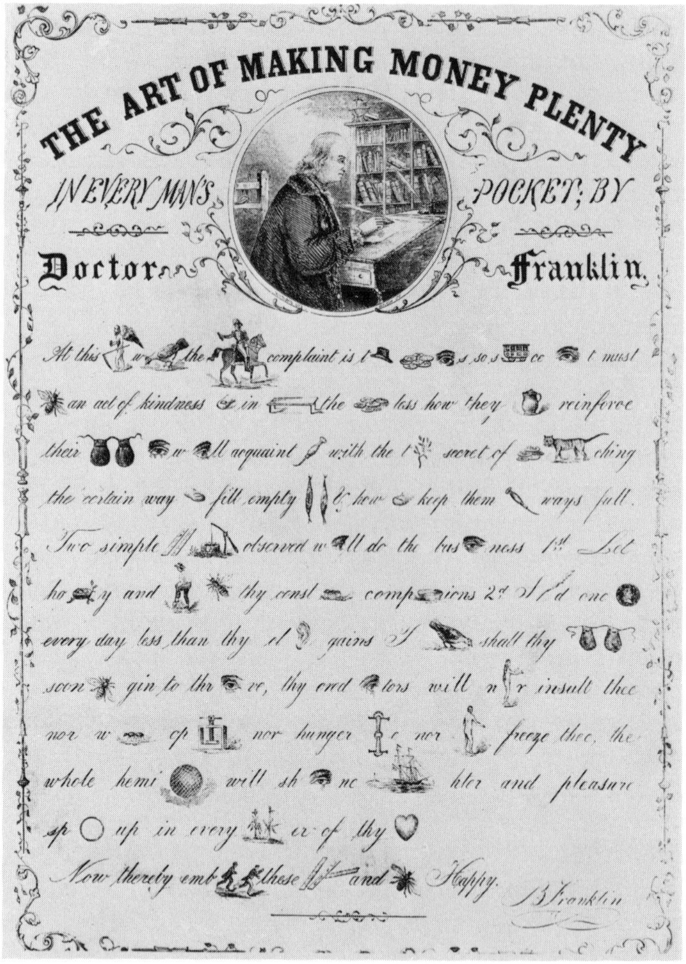

In order to learn "the art of making money plenty," the colonial reader had to interpret the puzzle of words and images presented by "Doctor Franklin" in this issue of *Poor Richard's Almanack*.

through the course less frequently, but he always carried the ivory tablet with him, and believed that "tho' I never arrived at the Perfection I had been so ambitious of obtaining, but fell far short of it, yet I was made a better and a happier Man than I otherwise should have been, if I had not attempted it."

Franklin's printing business continued to prosper. He sponsored another apprentice, Louis Timothee, sending him to South Carolina to take over the shop that had been run by Whitmarsh, who died of yellow fever in September 1733. Among other efforts at self-improvement, in addition to the table of moral virtues, Franklin taught himself three new languages: Latin, Spanish, and Italian.

In 1735, Franklin used the *Pennsylvania Gazette* to propose and promote a fire protection society. He had been in Boston in 1733 for a visit and had seen how a volunteer fire company operated there. He wrote an article on the question for the newspaper, and in a short time a group of 30 men was formed, calling itself the Union Fire Company, each member of which supplied himself with a leather bucket and other tools for fighting fires. The company met regularly, coordinated its efforts, discussed the problems associated with fire fighting, bought new equipment with the fines imposed for absences from meetings, and when too many new members wished to join, advised them on starting a second and a third company. Soon there were many such fire companies throughout Philadelphia, and the city was considerably safer from the dangers of fire. The Union Fire Company exemplified Franklin's belief in the value of voluntary cooperation for social benefit.

After instituting fire-fighting companies, Franklin began to lobby for better police protection. The present system involved constables in each of the city's wards, who sought volunteers from among the men of the neighborhood to take turns patrolling the streets at night. Those who did not want to take their turn paid the constable to hire a substitute for the night, but often the money went into the constable's own pocket, or he hired a local drunkard for the price of a drink. Either way, the result was not very effective. Franklin proposed a system of paid night watchmen instead. It took longer for Philadelphia to adopt this plan than it had taken to form the fire companies, but finally, in 1752, a professional police force was instituted.

Poor Richard speaks with the authentic voice of early American capitalism.
—ESMOND WRIGHT
Franklin biographer

In 1736, Franklin was engaged to print the currency of New Jersey. From July to September he worked in Burlington to do so. Counterfeiting was widespread at the time, and Franklin set his mind to the task of devising a way to prevent it. What he came up with was a brilliant innovation called "nature printing." He used a leaf from a tree, with its intricate and completely unique outline and pattern of veins, to make an impression in a soft material, and then he used that impression to cast a metal plate that could be inked and pressed to paper to imprint the leaf's image. The detailing of this singular image would then be so fine that it was beyond the ability of the most skilled engraver to copy it and counterfeit the money. The New Jersey currency, with its prominent leaf image, was also, incidentally, quite beautiful.

Franklin suffered the devastating loss of his second son, Francis Folger Franklin, in 1736, when the child was four. Franky, as he was called, had contracted smallpox. Franklin was long to regret that he had neglected to have his son inoculated. Inoculation was a new and controversial practice at the time: It involved giving a person a small dose of a virus, enough to stimulate the person's body to create antibodies to the disease but not enough to give the person the disease itself. Still, a few people did contract the disease from inoculation, so it was a calculated risk. When Franklin had worked for his

By 1735, Franklin's original printing shop on Market Street in Philadelphia was just one of a number of shops sponsored and financed by Franklin and situated in such diverse locations as South Carolina, New York, and the West Indies.

brother James on the *New England Courant*, they had campaigned against inoculation, which was promoted in Boston by Cotton Mather, the Puritan minister. Since that time, Franklin had come to understand that inoculation was a beneficial medical practice, but he had not yet had his son inoculated. After Franky's death, rumors circulated that he had died as a result of inoculation, so Franklin wrote a brief notice in the *Gazette* contradicting the rumors and urging other parents to have their children inoculated and thereby avoid the sorrow that he was experiencing.

In 1735, Franklin donned the hat of a fire fighter when he founded the Union Fire Company of Philadelphia, one of the many public projects the civic-minded Pennsylvanian would undertake during his lifetime.

Franklin suffered one of his few serious business failures in 1741. He announced his plan to establish the first American magazine. When Andrew Bradford responded to this announcement by starting his own magazine, Franklin accused him of stealing the idea and retaliated by undercutting Bradford's price. His first issue of *The General Magazine and Historical Chronicle* was published on February 16, 1741, and appeared monthly for six issues thereafter. But it failed to catch on, and Franklin folded it after the sixth issue.

At about the same time, however, Franklin had one of his most well-known successes: the Pennsylvania fireplace, also known as the Franklin stove. An early version was advertised for sale on February 5, 1741, but Franklin tinkered with the design for several years. Its purpose was to heat rooms more effectively and economically; its method was to circulate the air warmed by the fire rather than allow it to rise up the chimney directly, and thus to heat the room by convection rather than simply by radiant heat. He turned his design over to Robert Grace, the friend who had loaned him the money to buy out Meredith, his former partner in the printing enterprise. Grace operated a foundry, where he began manufacturing the iron stove, which Franklin promoted by writing and publishing a pamphlet called *An Account of the New-Invented Pennsylvania Fire-Place*. Franklin did not patent his invention, considering it instead a gift for the public benefit, and so other manufacturers copied his design and profited by the sales. But its widespread

Franklin was a versatile and prolific writer. Along with *Poor Richard's Almanack*, he wrote and published various pamphlets, a magazine, and numerous articles for his own newspaper, the *Pennsylvania Gazette*.

success increased Franklin's fame, as his name was forever attached to the stove.

The design of the stove had involved careful scientific reasoning about the conservation and transmission of heat and the behavior of hot air. Franklin was becoming increasingly interested in science, and in order to make time for more research and experimentation, he entrusted his business to an apprentice named David Hall, who joined him in 1744. (Hall was sent to him by William Strahan, a London printer with whom Franklin often did business.) Franklin proposed to set Hall up in another colony, but Hall instead remained in Philadelphia with Franklin and quickly became a trusted associate. As Franklin's business therefore demanded less constant attention, his scientific pursuits took precedence.

In the late spring of 1743, Franklin had made a trip to New England, and while he was in Boston he attended lectures on electricity given by Archibald Spencer. These "lectures" were more in the way of a popular entertainment: Spencer, like other "electricians" of the day, traveled about with a rudimentary apparatus, selling tickets to shows at which he performed electrostatic demonstrations — giving people shocks, making sparks leap in the dark, and otherwise impressing the public with what seemed like magical effects. Franklin's meeting with Spencer was a decisive moment in his life; it stirred his interest in the field of electricity, in which Franklin's own most important research would be done. At Franklin's invitation, Spencer came to Philadelphia to give his demonstrations, and Franklin was so charmed and interested in electricity that he bought Spencer's equipment and began conducting experiments himself.

French "scientists" conduct an experiment on the passage of electricity through the human body. Franklin became aware of such research in 1743; he acquired his own electrical apparatus and was soon deeply involved in the study of electricity.

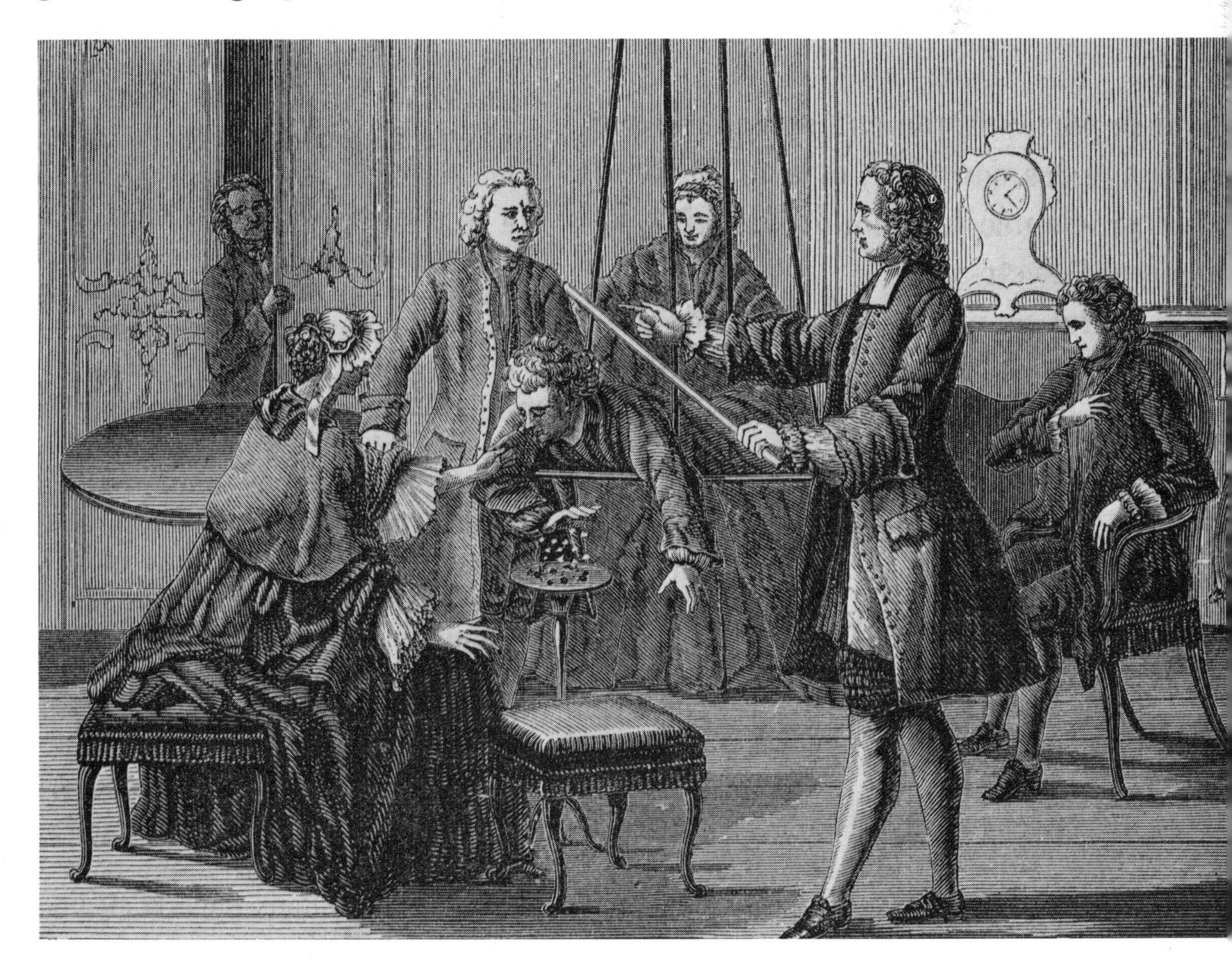

4

"A House Thus Furnished"

> ***The very heavens obey him, and the Clouds yield up their Lightning to be imprisoned in his rod.***
>
> —WILLIAM PIERCE
> Georgia delegate to the Constitutional Convention, on Franklin

During the mid-to-late 1740s, Franklin was immersed in electrical experimentation. Having bought Archibald Spencer's apparatus in 1744, Franklin asked a British correspondent, the amateur scientist Peter Collinson, to send him additional materials and information for his experiments. In 1745, Collinson sent a pamphlet describing recent German experiments in electricity, along with a glass tube that could be used to collect an electrical charge. On May 25, 1747, Franklin sent Collinson a detailed report of his experiments, and Collinson read it to the Royal Society of London, the most important scientific body of the day. In this report, Franklin announced his discovery that a pointed metal rod would draw off the charge from an electrified object when the point was brought near the object. Electricity, Franklin hypothesized, was "an Element diffused among, and attracted by other Matter, particularly by Water and Metals."

By performing an experiment with three people, the first of whom rubbed a glass tube with silk to

By 1745, Franklin had achieved financial success and had "no other tasks than such as I shall like to give myself." In later years, "uninterrupted by the little cares and fatigues of business," he devoted his time almost exclusively to the study of electricity, intent on producing "something for the common benefit of mankind."

charge it with static electricity, the second of whom received the spark of electricity from the tube, and each of whom then seemed to be electrified with respect to a third person, Franklin discovered that there were positive and negative electrical charges. Previously, scientists had thought there were two different kinds of electricity; Franklin showed that it was the same thing, only taking two different forms — plus and minus. Such an idea, commonplace today, was revolutionary then.

The glass tube was soon replaced by a more sophisticated apparatus for collecting electrical charges, the Leyden jar. A static charge stored in a Leyden jar could be made to give off sparks, attract light objects, and so forth. Curious neighbors often came to watch Franklin's experiments, so he engaged some friends to conduct demonstrations for the public. This enabled him to get on with his research.

In 1749, Franklin constructed the first primitive battery out of panes of lead and glass, with which he could collect a stronger electrical charge — strong enough to be sent through the water of Philadelphia's Schuylkill River, he claimed, to be drawn out on the other side where it would be used to light a container of alcohol. He also used electricity to kill a turkey and then to light a fire over which to roast the bird. Along with his serious scientific interests, Franklin was quite willing to further his rapidly growing celebrity status by astounding the public with such wizardly feats.

On April 29, 1749, Franklin wrote to an associate that he had a "new Hypothesis for explaining . . . Thunder-gusts." He argued that the particles of water forming clouds contained electrical charges and that clouds formed over the ocean had more electricity than clouds formed over land. Differently charged clouds were therefore attracted to one another and equalized their electricity by the passage of lightning between them. At other times clouds would discharge their electricity into church steeples, tall buildings, masts of ships, or big trees. In November, in his journal of experiments, Franklin noted the many similarities between lightning and

In 1749, in his laboratory at home, Franklin fashioned the first battery, a lead and glass device that could hold a strong electrical charge.

electricity, explicitly proposed that they were one and the same, and called for an experiment to be made to prove this hypothesis.

On March 2, 1750, Franklin proposed to Collinson that pointed rods attached to the tops of buildings might attract electricity from storm clouds, and thus, by diverting the lightning, protect structures from damage. By July, he had devised an experiment that would clarify the relationship between lightning and electricity: He proposed that during a thunder-and-lightning storm a sort of sentry box be placed on top of a hill or on a steeple, with a pointed rod extending above it and a wire leading from the rod down to the man inside the box. If the man started giving off sparks, Franklin surmised, that would prove that the rod was conducting electricity down to his body. Franklin believed the man would be in no danger.

In December 1750, when he was about to electrocute an unfortunate turkey with the accumulated

Flying a silk kite during a thunderstorm, Franklin and an assistant wait for the metal wire attached to the kite to be struck by lightning; the resulting electrical charge would flow down the kite string and be caught in the Leyden jar on the left.

electrical charge in two large Leyden jars, Franklin accidentally shocked himself instead of the turkey. He was knocked unconscious and a seizure was induced. He gradually returned to consciousness as his body shook on the floor with violent spasms. He felt numb in his arms and in the back of his neck until the next day. Undaunted, and determined, as always, to put all of his discoveries to practical use, Franklin was soon administering electrical shocks to paralyzed people. These shocks would, he later wrote, afford some temporary improvement to the paralytics — their limbs would feel warmth and a tingling sensation, and they could move them somewhat more freely — but he never effected a complete cure of paralysis, and his patients soon found that the severity of the shocks was worse than the difficulty of the paralysis.

In June 1752, Franklin arranged for a kite made of a silk handkerchief stretched over a frame of cedar strips to be flown in a thunderstorm. A pointed metal wire was fastened to the top of the kite to attract electricity, which was then conducted by the wet silk and the wet string down to the ground, where a key was fastened to the string. Franklin, by this time well aware of the danger involved, specified that a silk ribbon be attached to the string where the key was suspended, and that a person hold the silk ribbon inside a door or window, where it could be kept dry and thereby insulate the person from the electricity streaming down the string and into the key. From the key, then, the electrical charge could be drawn off into a Leyden jar, or used to kindle a flame in alcohol or to perform some other demonstration. Franklin kept the successful result of the kite experiment secret for a few months. Only in October did he publish a report of it in the *Gazette*, and in his almanac for the coming year he advocated and described the use of a lightning rod to protect houses and other structures during storms: "A House thus furnished will not be damaged by Lightning, it being attracted by the Points, and passing thro the Metal and into the Ground without hurting any Thing."

Franklin put a lightning rod on top of his own house, extending about nine feet above the chimney. Rather than grounding the rod in the earth outside the house, however, he brought a wire leading from it through the roof and down the stairwell, where he attached bells to the wire. When a cloud passed overhead, and the rod and wire were electrified, the bells would ring to remind him to collect some of the charge into Leyden jars. One night, he reported, he was awakened not by the bells, as usual, but by a loud crackling noise. He went down and discovered a fantastic sight: The electrical charge was so strong that instead of ringing the bells it was passing visibly from bell to bell, sometimes in large sparks and sometimes "in a continued, dense, white stream, seemingly as large as my finger, whereby the whole staircase was in lightened as with sunshine, so that one might see to pick up a pin." In that moment Franklin caught a glimpse of the bright future he had helped to fashion with his research into electricity.

Franklin would continue his experiments, but he had made his essential discoveries: positive and negative electricity, the relationship between lightning and electricity, and the use of pointed rods to attract electricity from clouds. His attention had already begun to turn again to public affairs — to new leadership roles, new philanthropic efforts, and new social and political problems.

In 1747, while still deeply involved in scientific research, Franklin had published a pamphlet, *Plain Truth*, in which he warned that Pennsylvania was vulnerable to raids by Spanish and French privateers (armed sailing vessels, privately owned but authorized by their government to take action against the shipping of a hostile nation). To help defend Pennsylvania from such raids, Franklin organized a voluntary militia. He refused to accept the position of colonel in the militia, saying that he had no military experience. Instead, he served as a common soldier.

By 1749, Franklin had been elected to the Common Council of Philadelphia and named a justice of the peace. During that same year, Franklin wrote and published a pamphlet called *Proposals Relating to the Education of Youth in Pennsylvania*, in which he called for the creation of an academy and outlined the curriculum that he considered proper for such a school. The result of his proposal was the founding of the Philadelphia Academy, an institution that grew to become the present University of Pennsylvania. It formally opened on January 7, 1751. Franklin published another pamphlet, *Idea of the English School*, proposing in some detail the year-to-year course of study at the academy. Franklin's approach to education was typically practical: The emphasis was on reading, writing, and speaking the English language rather than Latin or the various ancient languages that were taught in other schools. The purpose of conducting studies in English was to make the students into useful citizens rather than learned scholars.

He found electricity a curiosity and left it a science.

—CARL VAN DOREN
Franklin biographer

Also in 1751, the Pennsylvania Assembly passed a bill Franklin had proposed founding the Pennsylvania Hospital. As was his usual practice, Franklin first wrote about this proposal in the *Pennsylvania Gazette*; his "Appeal for the Hospital" was a two-

Private Benjamin Franklin patrols the Philadelphia wharf. Although it was Franklin who organized Pennsylvania's volunteer militia, he refused an officer's rank, preferring to serve as a common soldier instead.

part essay, printed in successive issues, in which he argued that by a cooperative effort — such as the founding of a hospital — Philadelphians could practice the virtues of Christian charity and care for the sick and poor more effectively than they could individually. Franklin gave credit for the hospital idea to a friend of his, Dr. Thomas Bond, but it was Franklin whose influence made the idea a reality. He accomplished this with an innovative piece of legislation, which directed that the assembly would contribute a certain sum of money to found the hospital if that same sum could also be raised from voluntary donations. This method of matching funds has been used successfully ever since. The hospital was to open on February 6, 1752.

Franklin was elected to the Pennsylvania Assembly on May 9, 1751, and therefore relinquished his position as clerk of the assembly to his son William. He would be reelected annually until 1764. In July 1751, he initiated a proposal to merge the many fire companies of the city into a single one; and on September 7, representatives of the companies met to form the Philadelphia Contributionship. Franklin was elected an alderman of Philadelphia on October 1.

Taking a trip through New England in the summer of 1753, Franklin's scientific achievements were rewarded when both Harvard and Yale Universities conferred honorary degrees on him, on July 25 and September 12, respectively. Franklin was especially gratified by these honors; he had been disappointed as a young man when his father could not afford to send him to college. In November

his genius was further recognized when the Royal Society of London awarded him its Copley Medal — the most prestigious scientific award in the world at the time—for his work on electricity.

The three main concerns to occupy Franklin's political agenda during the next few years were Indian affairs, paper currency, and the authority of the Penn family as proprietors of Pennsylvania. These issues were interrelated. The heirs of the founder of Pennsylvania, William Penn, lived in England and considered their vast landholdings in Pennsylvania a source of revenue; they received rents from them and the value of the land itself was rising. At the same time, they paid no taxes on their lands and therefore contributed nothing to the cost of defending the colony. What made this situation especially irksome to Pennsylvanians was the new danger posed by restless Indian tribes on the frontier (the

British general Edward Braddock, mortally wounded in a July 1755 battle against the French and Indians near Fort Duquesne, Pennsylvania, is helped onto one of the wagons supplied to him by Benjamin Franklin.

Franklin likened the colonies to a snake: Divided they would die, but unified they could survive. A 1756 cartoon by Franklin exhorts the colonies to unify as a defense against a French invasion.

region that is now western Pennsylvania and eastern Ohio). The Indians in this area were being squeezed between the English settlers gradually pushing westward past the Allegheny Mountains and the French moving in on the western side and settling in the Ohio Valley. Both the English and the French sought to keep the Indians pacified by bribing them with gifts.

The expense of defending the frontier and bribing the Indians was considerable, and the assembly demanded that the Penns contribute to this expense; after all, it was their land that was being defended. When the Penns refused to pay taxes, the assembly chose to print paper money to help support the costs. The governor, who was appointed by the Penns, resisted the effort to introduce paper money. Meanwhile, the French were building forts in the Ohio country. The vulnerability of the English settlements to both the French and the Indians, and the lack of support from the Penns and from the king of England, led Franklin, along with other colonial leaders, to consider the possibility of a defensive union among the colonies themselves.

In May 1754, Franklin printed an account in the *Gazette* of the building of a French fort at Duquesne, on the fork of the Ohio River, and described in vivid terms the havoc that the French were sure to wreak on the frontier as they built more forts.

"The Confidence of the French in this Undertaking," Franklin wrote, "seems well-grounded on the present disunited State of the British Colonies, and the extreme Difficulty of bringing so many different Governments and Assemblies to agree in any speedy and effectual Measures for our common Defence and Security." Against the evident French plans to attack and destroy British settlements, Franklin urged, the only defense was to unify the various colonies. Accompanying this article was a cartoon Franklin drew; underscored with the warning "Join, or Die," it depicted a snake cut into pieces, each piece representing one of eight British colonies. The message was perfectly clear. More than 20 years before the American Revolution, Franklin was imploring the colonies to "hang together."

The way to secure peace is to be prepared for war.
—BENJAMIN FRANKLIN

To make the proposed defensive union a reality, a congress was held at Albany, New York, in June and July 1754. Representatives of seven colonies — including Franklin for Pennsylvania — sought to form an alliance with the Iroquois Indians and to cooperate in military measures to defend the frontier. On July 2, the congress voted to form a union, and Franklin proposed a plan that was approved on July 10. Unhappily, when the Albany Plan of Union was sent to the various colonies for ratification, they all rejected it. Even Pennsylvania refused to approve it, wary of a union that was to be headed by a president general appointed in England. The British government likewise rejected the plan as they did not like its provision for a grand council to be elected by the assemblies of the various colonies. Franklin would long regret what he considered to be the shortsighted objections to this plan. He believed that if it had been instituted, the colonies could have defended themselves, no British troops would have been sent to the colonies, and the resentment among Americans toward the British troops and the taxation to which the colonies were subjected to support these troops would not have led the colonies to their eventual revolution against the British crown — in short, the "bloody contest" of the American Revolution would never have happened, and many lives would have been spared.

The Siege of Troy
is here

5

Cool Thoughts

In the spring of 1757, the Pennsylvania Assembly appointed Franklin their agent to England; he was to go to London to seek a resolution to the dispute between the assembly and the Penns. Franklin went to New York on April 4 to meet a ship that would take him across the Atlantic. His son William, then 27 years old, accompanied him. The ship, the *General Wall*, was delayed repeatedly by the earl of Loudoun, commander in chief of British forces in America. French men-of-war were believed to be cruising in the vicinity, and Franklin had no choice but to wait impatiently for departure. The ship, once allowed to sail, was nearly wrecked on the Scilly Isles, off England's Land's End, and when Franklin and the other passengers finally came ashore, they went immediately to church to give thanks for their safety. Franklin's practical outlook and skepticism are evident in the letter he wrote at that time to his wife: "Were I a Roman Catholic, perhaps I should on this occasion vow to build a chapel to some saint; but as I am not, if I were to vow at all, it should be to build a lighthouse."

When I meet him anywhere, there appears in his wretched countenance a strange mixture of hatred, anger, fear, and vexation

—BENJAMIN FRANKLIN
on Thomas Penn

Franklin soon sent off the 1758 almanac to David Hall in Philadelphia and then settled back into a comfortable life in London. He was glad to be back,

The London that Benjamin Franklin returned to in 1757, as depicted here by William Hogarth, was a teeming, bustling, and sometimes chaotic city. Upon arriving, Franklin and his son William eagerly immersed themselves in the unlikely mixture of high and low culture that constituted British society.

for he had come to admire the British and their way of life. And he was no longer an anonymous young printer's apprentice scraping by in a strange city, as he had been during his previous stay in London. He was now a successful businessman from Philadelphia, a scientist whose reputation preceded him, and a diplomatic agent on an important international mission. In these prestigious roles he had returned to what was now the largest city in Europe (750,000 inhabitants) and the capital of Anglo culture.

Franklin found lodgings for himself and William in a rooming house at 7 Craven Street belonging to a widow, Mrs. Margaret Stevenson. Mrs. Stevenson would thereafter be Franklin's landlady, and soon she was his friend; he became an integral part of her household and practically a member of her family. He took a special interest in her daughter Mary (called Polly), who was bright and charming and would remain devoted to him for the rest of his life.

> ***I wish every Kind of Prosperity to my Friends, and I forgive my enemies.***
>
> —BENJAMIN FRANKLIN
> on leaving America in 1764

Franklin and William outfitted themselves with fashionable clothes and wigs and plunged into the thriving London society. William was soon engaged in studying the law, whereas his father resumed his love affair with London. He renewed old friendships, was introduced to prominent men, and began frequenting the alehouses, clubs, and coffeehouses in which much of the social life and political action was taking place.

In addition to immersing himself in the social and intellectual life of London, Franklin went to work on behalf of the Pennsylvania Assembly to try to negotiate its dispute with the Penns. He went to see Lord Granville, president of the Privy Council (the king's closest advisers), and was alarmed when Granville told him that the king was the supreme lawgiver to the colonies. Franklin had thought that the laws for the colonies were to be made by the elected legislatures of the colonies themselves and then submitted for the king's approval. Granville, however, claimed that the king could dictate law for the colonies without their consent. This fundamental disagreement would lead the colonies to revolt

nearly 20 years later, and Franklin may very well have felt a sense of foreboding as he listened to Granville.

Franklin's immediate task was to appeal to the new king, George III, against the Penns, who were unfairly exempted from taxation in Pennsylvania. They held huge tracts of land but paid no taxes on them; the cost of defending the colony was great but the Penns contributed nothing to those costs. Franklin had some success in getting the Penns' estates taxed, but not much. He began to hope, however, that he might eventually be able to overturn the Penns' authority altogether and have Pennsylvania receive a charter of government from the king, as most of the other colonies had. Then the governor would be appointed by the king, rather than by a family of wealthy private citizens who enjoyed the unusual privilege of governing the colony from afar. It was not perfectly clear that royal government, in place of proprietary government, would be a great improvement — Lord Granville's assertion of the king's total authority made that clear. But Franklin's judgment was that it would be easier to deal with the king and Parliament than with the Penns, and so he directed his efforts toward that end.

Two English gentlemen discuss politics while a group of merrymakers carries on at a corner table. Much of London's political and intellectual life took place in eating and drinking establishments such as this one, allowing Franklin to satisfy several different appetites at once.

King George III, who assumed Great Britain's throne in 1760, was much admired by Franklin at first. As friction between England and the American colonies intensified, however, the monarch fell from favor with Franklin and his fellow colonists.

Hoping to sway public opinion, and thus to put pressure on his adversaries to compromise, Franklin began to mount a campaign in the press on behalf of the colonies. His newspaper articles, appearing frequently in the London papers during the subsequent years of political contention, were masterful examples of satirical argument. Their consistent assumption was that the colonists were British subjects — therefore entitled to all the political rights that such a status ought to confer — and that the king should act to guarantee those rights. (Franklin sincerely believed at the time that it was in the colonies' interest to remain a part of the British Empire, and his involvement with London society reinforced that belief.)

Franklin's political mission had been partly successful, but he could see no further advantage to be gained by staying on. He enjoyed his associations with scientists and philosophers, but he had a family in Philadelphia that desired his return, and his obligations there laid a greater claim on him than the pleasures of London. His friend William Strahan, the printer, tried to persuade Franklin to stay by offering to marry his son to Franklin's daughter

Sally, and Franklin passed this proposal on to Deborah in a letter. But Deborah refused to come to England or to part with her child. In August 1762, Franklin reluctantly left London for Portsmouth, where he awaited a ship to take him to Philadelphia.

William Franklin remained in London, where he had fathered an illegitimate son in 1760 and was engaged to marry a wealthy young woman named Elizabeth Downes. The marriage took place on September 4, 1762; on September 9, William was appointed royal governor of New Jersey. The English authorities may have thought that by giving William the unexpected appointment (he had been seeking only the deputy secretaryship of South Carolina, not a governorship), they would influence his father in the future. In fact, they had only provided what would eventually become a source of bitter enmity between Franklin and his only surviving son, who, as royal governor, would remain loyal to England and the king during the Revolution.

Franklin returned to Philadelphia to find his wife and family in a new house across the street from their old address. He was soon as busy as ever with

William Franklin is introduced to the highborn and wealthy Elizabeth Downes of London. On September 4, 1760, Franklin and Downes were married; five days later, Franklin was appointed royal governor of New Jersey.

politics, business affairs, and civic duties. As postmaster general of the colonies (he had been appointed to the position in 1756), he undertook extensive travels to inspect post offices and do what he could to improve mail service. His travels in this effort enabled him to see many old friends and family members, too — in New Jersey he saw William and his bride, who arrived in February 1763 to take up the governorship. Franklin's postal inspections brought him as far south as Virginia and as far north as Maine. Altogether he was gone from home for seven months. His longest visit was two and a half months in Boston, his childhood home, where he was detained in part because he dislocated his shoulder when he fell from a horse.

After a lifetime in rented houses, Franklin and his wife were building a large new house on Market Street in Philadelphia, three stories tall and a fitting home for an important public man. In the house he would display, among the many elegant acquisitions he had purchased in London, the musical instrument he had invented just before his return. He called it the armonica. It consisted of a set of bell-shaped glasses, in graduated sizes, lying one inside another along an iron rod that pierced their center and supported them above a tray. A foot pedal operated a mechanism that turned the glasses on the

Colonial postmaster general Benjamin Franklin takes a break from his appointed rounds and accepts some refreshment from a young lady. Franklin greatly improved the efficiency of the colonial postal system during his tenure as postmaster general.

Franklin sets his foot to the pedal and his wetted fingers to the glass bells of the armonica, the musical instrument he invented during his 1757–62 sojourn in Great Britain.

rod, while wet fingers applied to the spinning rims of the glasses produced beautiful tones. The instrument never met with widespread popularity, although Mozart and Beethoven composed for it, and the French psychic healer Anton Mesmer found it useful in his therapy.

While the house was under construction, Franklin's involvement with less trivial matters once again occupied his energies. He had been reelected to the Pennsylvania Assembly every year during his absence, but the political scene had changed during that time. The Quakers were less powerful now, whereas Scotch-Irish settlers on the violent frontier were more politically active. The French and Indian War had been fought, and now the entire continent east of the Mississippi was under British control. The friendship of the Native Americans had been cultivated by both the French and the English while those nations were at war in North America, but after the war ended the Indians had been neglected.

Chief Pontiac of the Ottowa Indians parleys with frontiersmen in the early 1760s. Relations between the Indians and white settlers were deteriorating steadily, and in 1763, Pontiac led a violent uprising that flared for three years.

White settlers were pushing westward, and the Indians resisted displacement. In the spring of 1763, Chief Pontiac led the Ottawa Indians in an uprising that would last for three years. Franklin's general attitude had been that whenever possible, the Indians and their demands should be met with negotiation, tactful accommodation, and bribery — until the Pontiac rebellion occurred, at which point he argued that the Indians should be dealt "some severe Blows" to demonstrate the white colonists' serious intentions.

One particular episode of racist, anti-Indian violence, however, deeply offended Franklin's sense of justice — a sense of justice that was to become increasingly apparent during the upcoming decades of Franklin's life. In December 1763, a band of frontiersmen from Donegal and Paxton townships in Lancaster County, Pennsylvania, angered by Indian attacks and by their feeling that the assembly was not doing enough to defend them, took revenge by raiding a small village of peaceful Indians at Conestoga. The frontiersmen murdered 6 of the friendly Indians, and 2 weeks later the mob killed the 14 remaining ones, who had been brought to the workhouse in Lancaster for protection. When the assembly ordered the "Paxton Boys," as they were called, to stand trial, they began to march east, planning to attack a group of 140 Indians who had been taken for their own safety to Province Island, in the Schuylkill River near Philadelphia. The mob also threatened to kill several prominent Quaker leaders for being too lenient with the Indians.

In response to these events, Franklin wrote *A Narrative of the Late Massacres*, reviewing the occurrences on the frontier and lambasting the Paxton Boys for murdering the helpless Indians who had done no harm to anyone:

> These poor People [the Indians] have been always our Friends. Their Fathers received ours, when Strangers here, with Kindness and Hospitality. Behold the Return we have made them! — When we grew more numerous and powerful, they put themselves under our Protection. See, in the mangled Corpses of the last Remains of the Tribe, how effectually we have afforded it to them!

Franklin then organized a company of men to defend the city against the approaching mob. He refused the governor's offer of the army's command, choosing to serve as an artilleryman instead. He allowed the governor to use his house as a headquarters during the crisis, however, and, as usual, exercised considerable influence behind the scenes.

Colonial ladies and gentlemen take afternoon tea in the mid-1760s. Such scenes were common in colonial America, but as political unrest intensified, relaxed social gatherings like this one became rare in the colonies.

William Pitt, the earl of Chatham and member of Parliament. Franklin admired the British statesman and hoped that he would be sympathetic to colonial resistance to the Stamp Act.

When the mob neared Philadelphia, Franklin rode out with six men to meet the rioters at Germantown, just outside the city, and tried to persuade them to desist. Surprisingly, he convinced them to present their grievances and then to disperse. Seemingly amazed at his own audacity, Franklin wrote a friend that "within four and twenty Hours, your old friend was a common Soldier, a Counsellor, a kind of Dictator, an Ambassador to the Country Mob, and on their Returning home, Nobody, again."

The unrest in Pennsylvania continued unabated, however, and Franklin began to yearn for the more "civilized" shores of England. "Every thing seems in this Country, once the Land of Peace and Order, to be running fast into Anarchy and Confusion," he wrote. Hoping still that the British king would grant a royal charter to Pennsylvania, he wrote another pamphlet, *Cool Thoughts on the Present Situation of Our Public Affairs*, in April 1764, supporting the assembly's recent resolution in favor of royal government. Elected speaker of the assembly in May, he petitioned the king to take over the government of Pennsylvania and remove the Penns from their position of power.

At the same time, the British Parliament was considering the notorious Stamp Act, which would impose taxes on sales of certain paper products in the colonies. Along with other colonial leaders, Franklin instructed his London agent, Richard Jackson, to lobby against the Stamp Act, arguing that the colonies ought not to be taxed by any legislature other than their own. The Stamp Act controversy was to play a major part in the sequence of events that would ultimately lead to war between Great Britain and the colonies.

In August and September, Franklin campaigned for reelection to the assembly, but he was subjected to a host of accusations that led to his defeat. In a vicious mudslinging campaign, unprecedented in Philadelphia politics, it was alleged that Franklin favored royal government because he hoped to be appointed governor, that he had misused public funds while he was serving in England, that his son

William's mother had been his former maidservant Barbara (and that he had buried her in an unmarked grave), and that he had once referred insultingly to German immigrants as "Palatine Boors." (The last accusation was quite true; Franklin had used the insult in a 1751 pamphlet.) The result of the nasty campaign was that Franklin lost his assembly seat on October 1, but his party held on to their majority, and they once again voted to appoint him agent to London. On November 7, he again left the agitated scene of Pennsylvania politics — and his wife — behind. This time, however, he was sailing toward a less hospitable Britain, and soon his task would be the more volatile diplomacy of war and peace.

Franklin sailed for England once again in late 1764; this time, however, he was to be confronted with a political system rife with corruption. The bribery and graft prevalent during this period are aptly illustrated in this engraving by William Hogarth.

6

An American Patriot in London

> ***My opinion has long been that Parliament has no Right to bind us by any kind of Law without our Consent.***
> —BENJAMIN FRANKLIN

Back in London, Franklin returned to his old Craven Street lodgings with Mrs. Stevenson, settling in on December 10, 1764. He was to remain in England for the next 10 years, not returning to the colonies until the musket shots that signaled the beginning of the revolutionary war had been fired at Lexington and Concord in Massachusetts. During those 10 years, Franklin underwent the most profound change in his political beliefs and loyalties.

When he arrived in London in 1764, Franklin was still an Anglophile; he was an admirer of the British king, George III, and he still believed that it was in the colonies' best interest to remain loyal to the Crown and to remain a part of the British Empire. By the time he left England in 1775, however, Franklin had become an uncompromising patriot, a man willing to sacrifice even familial loyalties to the cause of democracy and American independence. His reputation and public image in both England and the colonies were to undergo a corresponding transformation.

Franklin at work with the committee appointed by Congress to draft the Declaration of Independence. Franklin exerted a strong — and often unwelcome — editorial influence over the committee; the historic document was measurably strengthened by his moderate approach to the language.

Franklin (foreground) is quizzed by a member of Parliament on the floor of the House of Commons during the 1766 hearings on the Stamp Act. Franklin's cool and unperturbable performance during the two-week hearings resulted in the repeal of the hated legislation.

Franklin's first task in England was to forestall the Stamp Act, and he set to work immediately. With agents for other American colonies, he met with George Grenville, chancellor of the Exchequer, to lobby against the proposed taxes. Franklin's efforts were in vain, however, and the Stamp Act was passed by the House of Commons on February 27. The king gave his approval on March 22, and the act went into effect in the colonies on November 1. Now all colonial newspapers, legal documents, and business papers required an official stamp. The price of the stamps varied; the stamp for a liquor license, for example, was four pounds, while a copy of *Poor Richard's Almanack* required a two-pence stamp. The proceeds from the tax were to be used to finance the British military presence in North America.

In the colonies, reaction to the Stamp Act was strong and immediate. Outraged that they were being taxed by a legislature in which they had no representation — the English Parliament — the colonists offered a stiff resistance. There were boycotts of British goods and rioting in the streets. "Sons of Liberty"—anti-British agitators—fanned the flames of colonial discontent. Stamp officers were intimidated into abandoning their posts. Some had their houses looted and burned to the ground. Franklin, far away from the actual furor, underestimated colonial outrage and resolve and believed it was futile to resist the legislation. He nominated his friend John Hughes to be the distributor of the stamps in Pennsylvania, preferring to have the duties collected fairly and honestly, by someone trustworthy, rather than by some corrupt bureaucrat or agent of the British. This nomination, demonstrating a willingness to cooperate with the British government, led to rumors that Franklin actually supported the Stamp Act. In Philadelphia, protesters who thought Franklin had betrayed the colony marched on Franklin's house on September 16 and 17, threatening to burn it down. The stout Deborah Franklin armed herself and refused to flee the mob. Another mob, made up of Franklin's supporters, showed their readiness to defend the house, and the attackers dispersed. But Franklin was now seen as a Loyalist villain in the colonies, and his standing in the public eye was at a low point.

Franklin realized that the best way to salvage his reputation and political standing in the colonies was to secure the repeal of the Stamp Act. During the winter of 1765–66, he began sending letters and articles to various London newspapers. Rather than argue explicitly for his point of view, he used humor, exaggeration, and satire to make his case. Writing under the ironic pen name Pacificus, he urged the British government to send "Two Thousand Highlanders" (Scottish soldiers) to America, where several thousand Canadians and Indians would join them, forming an army that could overrun the colonies and suppress resistance to the Stamp Act:

> I would propose that all the Capitals of the several Provinces should be burnt to the Ground, and that they cut the Throats of all the Inhabitants, Men, Women, and Children, and scalp them, to serve as an Example. . . . No Man in his Wits, after such terrible Military Execution, will refuse to purchase stamp'd Paper. If any one should hesitate, five or six Hundred Lashes in a cold frosty Morning would soon bring him to Reason.

In another letter, Franklin went further; again with mock seriousness, he proposed that armies be sent

They [the Americans] think it extremely hard and unjust, that a body of men, in which they have no representatives, should make a merit to itself of giving and granting what is not its own, but theirs, and deprive them of a right they esteem of the utmost value and importance, as it is the security of all their other rights.

—BENJAMIN FRANKLIN speaking about the Stamp Act in the House of Commons

In 1774 he was known as "the most mischievous man in England," at least a thief and at worst a traitor; as the ringleader and puppet-master of rebellion, saying smooth things publicly in London but treacherously pulling the strings of rebellion in Boston.

—ESMOND WRIGHT
Franklin biographer

to all towns in the colonies in order to capture and castrate the males. This policy, Franklin explained, would effectively end the growing rebelliousness of the colonies.

In other letters to the press, Franklin took a gentler approach. In one piece he compared Great Britain to an eagle who, seeing a cat on the ground but mistaking it for a rabbit, swooped down and carried it off into the air. The cat (representing America in this parable) "set her Claws into the Eagle's Breast; who, finding his Mistake, opened his Talons, and would have let her drop; but Puss, unwilling to fall so far, held faster; and the Eagle, to get rid of the Inconvenience, found it necessary to set her down where he took her up." Franklin thus implied that America, like the abducted cat, would eventually compel Britain, the eagle, to return to the state of affairs that had existed before the Stamp Act and other oppressive measures were instituted.

Franklin's satirical writings had some effect, but it was his appearance at the House of Commons's hearings on the Stamp Act controversy in February 1766 that turned the tide and saw him transformed from villain to hero in the colonies. During the parliamentary hearings, Franklin answered 174 questions over a period of 2 weeks. The questions pertained to the Stamp Act and the situation in the colonies. The portly, bespectacled gentleman from Pennsylvania gave a masterful performance on the floor of the House of Commons. His answers to the questions were based on logic and common sense, an in-depth grasp of the economic situation in the empire, and an unshakable advocacy of the basic rights of the colonists. Soon members of Parliament found themselves nodding in agreement with Franklin's arguments, and on February 22, 1766, the House of Commons voted to repeal the Stamp Act. Now Franklin was the man of the hour, and glasses were raised in his name in taverns throughout the colonies. Although his victory was shortlived — the House of Commons voted to impose new duties on the colonies in 1767 — his reputation in America was restored.

Franklin did not allow his diplomatic chores to interfere with the more enjoyable and rewarding pursuit of his social, scientific, intellectual, and culinary interests. In 1767, he visited Paris and was presented to King Louis XV at the palace in Versailles. In 1768, Franklin designed a phonetic alphabet, in which he tried to make the written letters of the alphabet correspond more exactly to the sounds of spoken English. (He actually used this alphabet in a few letters he wrote to his landlady's daughter, Mary Stevenson, much to her dismay.) Franklin prepared a new edition of *Experiments and Observations on Electricity* in 1769, adding new discoveries (the first edition was published in 1751). He also found time to travel extensively throughout western Europe, eating and drinking liberally as he went.

In 1769, New Jersey appointed Franklin its London agent (Georgia had done so the previous year); in 1770, Massachusetts did the same. Franklin was now the leading negotiator for the American colonies, and although he continued to be the advocate

This cartoon of a funeral procession for the Stamp Act appeared in a London newspaper shortly after the act was repealed in February 1766. Despite the "death" of the Stamp Act, tensions between the colonies and the mother country continued to grow.

British redcoats open fire on a mob of Bostonians, killing five of them, on the evening of March 5, 1770. The Boston Massacre was one of a series of events that helped to sour Franklin's feelings toward England.

of moderation and conciliation between the colonies and the mother country, he also experienced a steadily increasing distaste for what he considered to be British imperial and parliamentary arrogance and corruption. His distaste was fueled by the news of the Boston Massacre, an incident in Boston in which British troops fired into a crowd of rowdy, snowball-throwing citizens, killing five of them. As his disillusionment with the British government grew, his writings in the British press began to take on a contemptuous tone, and his satire acquired a new savagery. In 1772, Franklin's changing political sentiments led him to take a controversial step in his capacity as colonial agent, a step that seems to indicate that he had come to a decision about where his true loyalties lay.

The die is cast. The colonies must triumph or submit.
—KING GEORGE III

Franklin obtained a packet of letters, written by the royal governor of Massachusetts, Thomas Hutchinson, and the lieutenant governor, Andrew Oliver. In these letters, which had been written to British authorities, Hutchinson and Oliver urged their superiors in London to take repressive measures against the rebellious colonies. (Royal appointees like Hutchinson and Oliver, and like William Franklin, were loyal to the king and were often at odds with the elected legislatures in the colonies.) Franklin decided to send these letters to the Massachusetts House, in order to inform the people's elected leaders that the royal governor had been working against them. The House decided, on the basis of this information, to petition the king to remove Hutchinson and Oliver from office.

Patriot Samuel Adams, gesturing wildly from the pulpit of Boston's Old South Church in December 1773, tries to make himself heard during the riotous town meeting that led to the Boston Tea Party.

At the same time, Hutchinson obtained a copy of one of Franklin's letters to the speaker of the Massachusetts House, Thomas Cushing. Hutchinson sent the copy to London, urging that Franklin be prosecuted as a traitor. Without the original letter, however, the prosecution could not take place, as only the original in Franklin's handwriting would be admissible as evidence in court. Nevertheless, when a hearing was held in London on the petition from Massachusetts, Franklin was publicly accused of having stolen the Hutchinson letters himself and denounced as a thief and a traitor. He was then stripped of his deputy postmastership, a position he had retained in Philadelphia even while absent. For the first time, Franklin had imperiled his own diplomatic standing in England in order to give the colonies political advantage. Although he defended his leak of the Hutchinson letters as an attempt to expose the mischief of their authors and thus reestablish honest dealings between the colonies and

Britain, it was clear that Franklin had lost a considerable amount of respect for his British hosts. The British, for their part, now perceived Franklin as a spy and an agitator.

In the colonies, and especially in Massachusetts, the hotbed of discontent, events began to gather momentum as they moved inevitably toward an open confrontation between colonists and British troops. On the evening of December 16, 1773, a group of Bostonians disguised as Indians boarded British tea-carrying vessels docked in Boston Harbor and dumped their cargo of tea overboard. This bold act of protest against the tax the British had imposed on tea imported to the colonies sent shock waves throughout the empire. News of what was already being called the Boston Tea Party reached London on January 20, 1774. There was outrage in Parliament. Franklin, in an attempt to defuse the situation, publicly condemned the act and offered to pledge his own personal fortune as compensation if Parliament would repeal the offending legislation. But his credibility had been undermined by the Hutchinson affair, and the British government assumed a hard-line stance and imposed new punitive laws—the Intolerable Acts—on Massachusetts.

Colonial Sons of Liberty, disguised as Indians and applauded by their fellow Bostonians, hurl cartons of tea off British ships and into the icy waters of Boston Harbor. In England, Franklin publicly condemned the "tea party," but his own patience with British arrogance was growing thin.

As tensions heightened, the American colonies formed the Continental Congress to coordinate colonial efforts to resist British domination. Through Franklin, the Congress petitioned the king for his intervention in the escalating disputes, but the time for moderation was over. As negotiations broke down, Franklin learned of his wife's death. Deborah had suffered a stroke on December 14, 1774, and had died 5 days later at age 66, having been apart from her husband for the last 10 years of her life. Parliament declared Massachusetts to be in rebellion on February 9, 1775, and Franklin, depressed

Virginians, gathered outside a village inn that happened to be named after King George III of England, read about the formation of the Continental Congress in the early spring of 1775.

by the death of Deborah and feeling that all hope for peace was lost, prepared to go home to Philadelphia.

It was a different Benjamin Franklin who disembarked at the Market Street Wharf in Philadelphia on a spring evening in 1775; and it was a different America to which he returned. At 70, Franklin had finally decided to sever his ties to mother England. He no longer considered himself a subject of the British king. The citizens of his homeland, in his absence, had arrived at the same decision and had taken the first irretrievable steps in that direction. At dawn on April 19, while Franklin was still at sea, 70 armed colonists had confronted a detachment of 800 British troops on Lexington Common in Massachusetts. Shots were fired, a skirmish ensued, and eight Americans were killed. The colonies were now in open rebellion: Across the countryside volunteer militias drilled; muskets and ammunition were hoarded; artillery was mustered. Franklin watched with approval as his homeland prepared for war.

It seems that I am too much of an American.
—BENJAMIN FRANKLIN
on leaving England in 1775

In less than a week, Franklin was in the thick of things. He was immediately chosen as a Pennsylvania delegate to the Second Continental Congress, which convened in Philadelphia on May 10. The other delegates — 70 in all — soon learned that the elderly Dr. Franklin had become something of a firebrand since he had last been in Philadelphia. And indeed, Franklin was at this point a step or two ahead of his colleagues. Whereas most of the other delegates were in favor of a cautious approach to the situation at hand and against any absolute assertions of independence as yet, Franklin was convinced that war was inevitable. He recommended that the colonies unite formally, declare themselves a sovereign state, and begin raising an army and forming alliances with some of Britain's enemies. Congress was unwilling to proclaim absolute independence, but they recognized the need for an army, and Franklin threw himself wholeheartedly into the organization of Pennsylvania's defense. At the same time, he drafted his Articles of Confederation and

Colonial minutemen exchange deadly volleys with British regulars on Lexington Common at dawn, April 19, 1775. The brief but bloody skirmish marked the beginning of the American Revolution.

Perpetual Union, asserting America's political sovereignty, which he submitted to Congress in July. Congress was still not as confident in the future of an independent America as Franklin was, however, and the Articles were not adopted. On August 23, King George III declared the colonies as a whole in rebellion, and on January 16, 1776, Franklin again argued in Congress for an instrument of confederation, but he was again defeated. The colonies were on the brink of independence, but Congress seemed unable to take the final step.

Although Congress was anything but decisive, Franklin embraced his radical patriotism with an unwavering — and even ruthless — determination. When his son, William, the royal governor of New Jersey, refused to renounce his loyalty to the king, he was deprived of his office and confined to his house by the New Jersey militia. In June, he was officially charged with treason, arrested, and thrown into prison in Connecticut. Although he was in a position to help his son, Franklin did nothing — he now considered William to be his enemy. William was to languish in prison throughout the war.

Finally, in June, Congress decided to appoint a committee to draft a statement of independence, even though delegates from Pennsylvania, New Jersey, New York, and South Carolina were still opposed to such a measure. Franklin was named to the committee, along with Thomas Jefferson, John Adams, Roger Sherman, and Robert Livingston. The committee chose the brilliant Jefferson of Virginia to compose a draft, which he produced within two days and which was then edited and revised — much to Jefferson's annoyance — by Franklin, Adams, and Congress. On July 1, after nine hours of exhausting and sometimes bitter debate, only two states, Pennsylvania and South Carolina, remained opposed to the motion for independence, while Delaware and New York were undecided. On July 2, 1776, Pennsylvania, South Carolina, and Delaware came over, and while New York delegates awaited instructions from home, a vote was taken. Twelve of the 13 colonies voted in favor of severing all bonds with Great Britain, and 2 days later, on July 4, 1776, Benjamin Franklin joined fellow members of Congress in signing the Declaration of Independence.

The five men who drafted the Declaration of Independence, from right to left: Benjamin Franklin of Pennsylvania, Thomas Jefferson of Virginia, John Adams of Massachusetts, Roger Sherman of Connecticut, and Robert Livingston of New York.

7

An American Patriot in Paris

> *[Franklin] loves his Ease, hates to offend and seldom gives any opinion till obliged to it. . . . Overwhelmed with hospitality . . . which keeps his mind in a constant state of dissipation . . . it is his constant Policy never to say 'Yes' or 'No' decidedly but when he can avoid it.*
>
> —JOHN ADAMS
> on Franklin in Paris

Four days after the Declaration of Independence was signed, Franklin was elected a Philadelphia delegate to the Pennsylvania Constitutional Convention, and a week after that he was chosen chairman of the convention. He began to oversee the process of organizing the former colony into an independent state. In the meantime, he continued as a major participant in national affairs. Congress met in Philadelphia, so Franklin was able to wear both hats — state and national — at once. He was also appointed postmaster general of the United States, thus regaining the position he had been stripped of in England as a result of the Hutchinson affair.

As chairman of the Pennsylvania Constitutional Convention, Franklin did little more than preside silently — and often only in spirit, for he was absent from the majority of meetings — over the proceedings. The tumultuous events of the past years had taken a toll, and he was exhausted from a recent military excursion to Canada — which had become a fiasco — and afflicted with various ailments of one

The Stars and Stripes — and the sun — rise over a new republic while the British Union Jack falls for the last time on the morning of October 10, 1881, at Yorktown, Virginia. Franklin did not fight in the revolutionary war, but the presence of the French troops that fought side by side with the Americans can be attributed to his skillful diplomacy in France.

kind or another. When he did attend the convention, other delegates frequently noticed that Franklin was fast asleep in his chair.

Although he seemed content to leave the bulk of the convention's work to the younger, more dynamic delegates, there were two issues that Franklin felt deserved his personal attention. First, having developed over the years a strong aversion to any mixing of church and state, he took a stand against a clause in the proposed Pennsylvania constitution that required members of the legislature to take an oath affirming their belief in God, heaven and hell, and the divine inspiration of the Scriptures. Second, Franklin refused to endorse legislation that made slavery a legal institution in Pennsylvania. The progressive and farsighted positions Franklin assumed on these issues show that his mind, if not his body, was still a step ahead of most of the other members of the legislature, who voted in favor of the proposals.

For dinner at two there was a joint of beef or veal or mutton, followed by fowl or game, with two sweets, two vegetables, pastry, hors d'oeuvres, butter, pickles, radishes, two kinds of fruit in winter, four in summer, two compotes, cheese, biscuits, bonbons, and ices twice a week in summer and once in winter.

—ESMOND WRIGHT
on Franklin's diet in
France

By the autumn of 1776, it had become apparent to Franklin and many other members of the fledgling American government that the British were ready to commit their military and economic resources to an extended war in North America. The American volunteer militia had inflicted heavy casualties on the British at the Battle of Bunker Hill, outside Boston, and a guerrilla band of Vermont mountain men — the "Green Mountain Boys" — under Ethan Allen had captured the strategically important Fort Ticonderoga, on Lake Champlain in upstate New York, but a subsequent attempt to liberate Canada from the British in the winter of 1775–76 had turned to disaster. And in August, the bulk of General George Washington's Continental Army had been virtually destroyed at the Battle of Long Island. Now, the tattered remains of Washington's forces were on the run in New Jersey, New York City was occupied by the British, and thousands of British reinforcements were disembarking on Staten Island.

If the United States was to wage a successful war against the most formidable military power in the world, it would need assistance. Congress therefore

Franklin, accompanied by John Adams (to his right) and Edward Rutledge, meets with England's Lord Howe on Staten Island late in the summer of 1776, in an unsuccessful attempt to negotiate a settlement between the colonies and the British.

dispatched Franklin and two others, Silas Deane and Arthur Lee, to France, where they would attempt to negotiate a treaty of alliance with, and solicit financial and military aid from, Great Britain's archrival.

Franklin sailed for France aboard the *Reprisal* on October 27, 1776. He took with him his two grandsons, Benjamin Franklin Bache (the eldest child of his daughter Sally and her husband, Richard Bache) and William Temple Franklin (illegitimate son of Franklin's illegitimate son William, the imprisoned former governor of New Jersey). Landing at Auray on December 3, he proceeded to Nantes, and then a week later to Paris, where he soon met with the French foreign minister, the comte de Vergennes.

Franklin's mission to France was of vital importance to the American cause. The infant United States simply did not have the resources to defeat Great Britain in a drawn-out conflict. Success would depend heavily on Franklin's skill at negotiating a treaty and enlisting economic and material aid from France. And maneuvering in the tangled diplomatic web that surrounded King Louis XVI would not be an easy task. But if the crucial and highly sensitive nature of Franklin's assignment caused him any stress or alarm, he did not show it. In fact, within a month of his arrival in France, it seemed that Franklin had embarked on an extended vacation rather than an all-important wartime mission. When the businesslike John Adams arrived in France a few months after Franklin, he found to his annoyance that the Pennsylvanian was happily ensconced in a private pavilion on the grounds of a luxurious hotel in Passy, where he was attended by eight servants, surrounded by British spies, and engaged in a social schedule that left him little time —it seemed to Adams—for diplomatic affairs.

Franklin could hardly resist the reception he was given upon his arrival in France. At age 70, he was a man with a large stomach and a large ego, and the French were more than willing to feed both. In France, Benjamin Franklin was what would be called, in today's parlance, a star. The French saw him as the personification of the ideas and values of the Enlightenment (the philosophical movement of the 18th century that was marked by an emphasis

Franklin studies French in preparation for his diplomatic mission to Paris. He sailed for France on October 27, 1776, and would remain there for almost 10 years.

The comte de Vergennes, French foreign minister under King Louis XVI, was to be Franklin's most important contact in Paris. Vergennes was dedicated not so much to American independence but rather to the defeat of the British.

on rationalism and a rejection of traditional social, religious, and political ideas), which were becoming popular in France at the time and would eventually change the face of French culture and the structure of French politics and society. To the French, Franklin was the perfect example of the idealized American. Self-made, both practical and intellectual, cultured yet unpretentious, urbane yet simple, Franklin represented the promise of the New World. He was at home in the salon and the laboratory; he was the advocate of republicanism and democracy; he was a man who could write scathing political satire and at the same time operate a printing press. The French dubbed him Bonhomme Richard and embraced him eagerly: He was inducted into various learned societies; showered with awards and honors; and banqueted regularly by leading French intellectuals, aristocrats, and courtiers. The general public followed his every move, scouring the papers for news of his activities, repeating with delight his latest witticisms. Rumors that the American had been sighted on a certain boulevard in Paris would generate huge crowds, whether Franklin was really there or not. In 1779, he wrote to his daughter in

Enlightenment writer Voltaire is crowned with laurels in his theater box after a performance of his tragedy *Irène* in Paris. According to Franklin biographer Esmond Wright, Franklin's "meeting and embrace with Voltaire at the Academy in 1778 were seen as a high point in the Enlightenment."

Philadelphia that his image was widely merchandised in France, appearing, for instance, on clay medallions that could be set in the lids of snuffboxes or worn on rings, and also in pictures, busts, and prints. His face, he wrote, was "as well known as that of the moon."

At his rooms in Passy, a suburb of Paris, Franklin held court. In his autobiography, John Adams described a typical day in the life of Bonhomme Richard:

> It was late when he breakfasted, and as soon as Breakfast was over, a crowd of carriages came to his . . . Lodgings, with all Sorts of People; some Philosophers, Accademicians and Economists; some of his small tribe of humble friends in the literary Way. . . . These Visitors occupied all the time, commonly, till it was time to dress to go to dinner. He was invited to dine abroad every day and never declined. . . . He went according to his Invitation to his Dinner and after that went sometimes to the Play, sometimes to the Philosophers but most commonly to visit those Ladies who were complaisant enough to depart from the custom of France so far as to procure Setts of Tea Geer as it is called and make Tea for him. After Tea the Evening was spent, in hearing the Ladies

> sing and play upon their Piano Fortes and other instruments of Musick, and in various Games as Cards, Chess, and Backgammon. . . . In these agreable and important Occupations and Amusements, the Afternoon and Evening was spent, and he came home at all hours.

Franklin was especially fond of the greater freedom in relations between the sexes in France and the greater participation of French women in politics and culture. Among his women friends, "those Ladies," as Adams described them, were Madame Brillon de Jouy (to whom he sent flirtatious letters and short, humorous prose sketches), the Comtesse d'Houdetot (mistress of Enlightenment philosopher Jean-Jacques Rousseau), and his favorite, the widow Madame Helvétius (her husband had been another philosopher), whose salon included France's finance minister and other leaders. (In 1778, Franklin proposed marriage to Madame Helvétius, perhaps only in the spirit of flattery, and was turned down.) Franklin delighted in the freedom of conversation, the liberal speculation, and the cultivated adventurousness of French intellectual life, and his years at Passy were among the happiest of his life. The French, he said, were "a most amiable [people] to live with."

It was understandable, then, that Franklin's fellow ministers — and especially the incorruptible Adams — thought him lazy, frivolous, dissipated, and inattentive to his diplomatic duties. After receiving word of the Continental Army's brutal winter at Valley Forge, where American soldiers froze to death and starved by the hundreds, the sight of Franklin dallying in Parisian salons was probably extremely distasteful to the other American diplomats. Had Franklin's mission failed, had he been unsuccessful in acquiring French economic and military aid for the United States, he would have been open to charges of gross negligence. He was, however, a skillful, clever, and above all an extremely persuasive diplomat, and his apparently casual approach to the job was in part a careful performance, well calculated to enlist French sympathy.

Admiring Parisians doff their hats to Bonhomme Richard on the streets of Paris. Franklin became the rage of all Paris; French statesman Turgot dubbed him the man who "seized the lightning from the sky and the scepter from tyrants."

Franklin's tactics worked: By January 13, 1777, he had received a verbal promise of 2 million livres from the comte de Vergennes, on the authorization of the French king. Soon French smuggling ships began depositing large caches of arms and ammunition on American shores. Franklin continued to extract large amounts of money from France as the war in America progressed. In January 1778, he obtained an additional 6 million livres, and in February, he successfully concluded negotiations for the Treaty of Amity and Commerce and the Treaty of Alliance between the United States and France. Franklin handled these negotiations brilliantly; he deftly played British and French diplomats off one another, to the ultimate advantage of the United States. On June 17, 1778, as a result of this treaty, France itself declared war on Britain; in 1779, Franklin received another 3 million livres; and by 1780 the French were openly sending troops and warships to the revolutionary forces. In 1782 and

Some of Franklin's colleagues strongly disapproved of his social life in France. John Adams, for example, wrote that the "Life of Dr. Franklin was a Scene of Continual dissipation."

Franklin, flanked by commissioners Silas Deane and Richard Henry Lee, looks on with satisfaction as the comte de Vergennes signs the Treaty of Alliance between France and the United States in February 1778.

again in 1783, Franklin obtained 6 million livres, bringing the total French contribution to over 20 million livres, a massive sum.

As French money and arms reached their destinations in the States, the tide of the war began to turn, slowly but steadily, in favor of the American forces. Although Franklin must have been happy as the news from America detailed victories for General Washington, he began to display a growing revulsion at the violence and waste of warfare. The pleasure he took in the good life was now tempered by a growing pessimism about the seemingly fundamental brutality of human beings. He continued to write and publish anti-British propaganda in the French press, but his private correspondence revealed mixed feelings about the war. Toward the end of the Revolution, he wrote to the English scientist Joseph Priestley:

> Men I find to be a Sort of Beings very badly constructed, as they are generally more easily provok'd than reconcil'd, more disposed to do Mischief to each other than to make Reparation, much more easily deceiv'd than undeceiv'd, and having more Pride and even Pleasure in killing than in begetting one another; for without a Blush they assemble in great armies at NoonDay to destroy, and when they have kill'd as many as they can, they exaggerate the Number to augment the fancied Glory; but they creep into Corners, or cover themselves with the Darkness of night, when

General George Washington, with French commanders Rochambeau and Lafayette, accepts the surrender of British general Cornwallis at Yorktown. As the British troops marched forward and relinquished their weapons, a military band played "The World Turned Upside Down."

> they mean to beget, as being asham'd of a virtuous Action. A virtuous Action it would be, if the Species were really worth producing or preserving; but of this I begin to Doubt.

In October 1781, after combined French and American forces won a decisive victory at Yorktown, Virginia, the British realized that they were beaten and began making overtures for peace. Congress appointed Franklin, Adams, and John Jay as commissioners to negotiate peace with Great Britain. Franklin once again found himself cast in his own favorite role, that of negotiator and conciliator.

Congress instructed its three agents to be flexible on all issues except one — Britain's recognition of the independence and sovereignty of the United States. Franklin, a most flexible man, not only remained steadfast on this matter, he conducted the discussions with an eye toward the future expansion of the United States into the West and the South. On November 30, 1782, preliminary articles of peace were signed. Clearly, Franklin, Adams, and Jay had gotten the best of the British negotiators: Britain officially recognized the complete independence of the United States and ceded generous boundaries to the new nation, from the Atlantic Ocean in the East to the Mississippi River in the

West, and from Florida in the South to the Canadian border in the North. Franklin's contributions to the peace negotiations were perhaps his greatest gift to the United States, for they helped to ensure a successful and independent future for the new nation and its citizens.

Franklin expressed his feelings about the end of the war in a letter to English scientist Sir Joseph Banks:

> I join with you most cordially in rejoicing at the return of Peace. I hope it will be lasting, and that Mankind will at length, as they call themselves reasonable Creatures, have Reason and Sense enough to settle their Differences without cutting Throats; for, in my opinion, there never was a good War, or a bad Peace.

The Treaty of Paris was officially ratified in Britain and in the United States, and the formal exchange of ratification took place in Paris on May 12, 1784. A year later, a tired Franklin received long-awaited permission from Congress to leave for home, and Thomas Jefferson took over as the United States minister to France. Franklin's health had deteriorated in recent years; he suffered increasingly from gout and bladder stones. The French queen, Marie Antoinette, furnished him with a litter borne by Spanish mules to take him from Passy to the port of Le Havre, where he would embark; this then, as the litter passed through the streets, was the last the French would see of Bonhomme Richard.

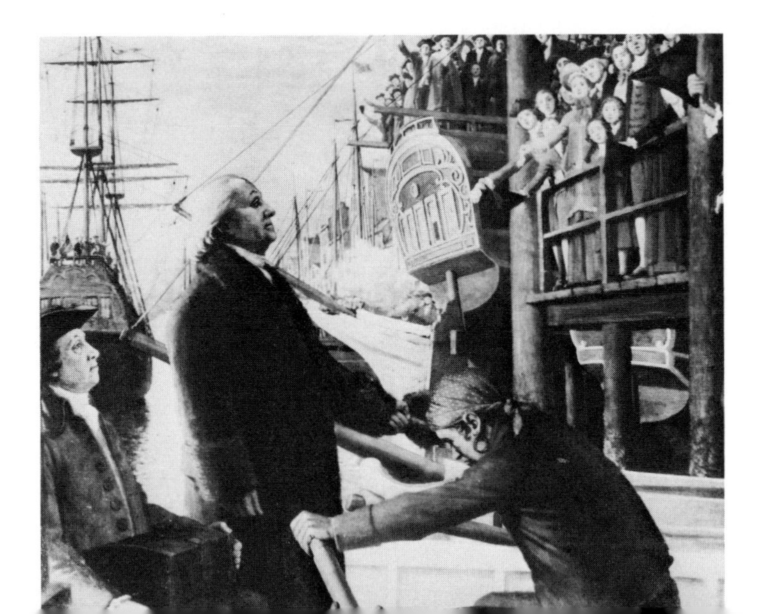

Huge crowds packed the Philadelphia waterfront to welcome home the hero Franklin on September 14, 1785. He stood proudly at attention as he was rowed ashore; cannons boomed salute after salute, church bells pealed, and the crowd cheered adoringly.

8

The Public Good

Franklin returned to Philadelphia a hero. He was immediately chosen president of the Pennsylvania Assembly, a largely honorary position, but one he enjoyed nevertheless. On days that the assembly met, he would preside congenially until about noon, often taking up these morning hours by telling humorous anecdotes and stories. At midday he would have lunch and then take a nap. He spent the evening hours receiving visitors, reading, planning new inventions, and writing. He still kept up a voluminous correspondence with acquaintances in America and Europe, and he had taken up work again on his unfinished autobiography, which he had begun in 1771. He also continued to publish his own articles, essays, and pamphlets.

In the spring of 1787, Franklin was chosen to be a member of the Constitutional Convention, which convened in Philadelphia on May 25. His health was failing — he was now 81 years old — and many of the other delegates believed that Franklin's condition would prevent him from attending the convention. But Franklin was not about to miss the gathering of men that would determine the new nation's future, and to the surprise of many, the elderly Pennsylvanian arrived, on a litter carried by four red-faced and sweating convicts, at the Pennsylvania

In all the range of his activities and all the publicity in which he lived, Franklin could often remain curiously uninvolved, never quite committing the whole man to the cause of the moment, quizzically looking in on himself from outside, and (one suspects) shaking with quiet laughter at the oddity of his own career.

—ESMOND WRIGHT
Franklin biographer

Benjamin Franklin was 79 years old when he returned to America for the last time. Although his health was failing and a new generation of leaders had come to the fore in the United States, the elderly Pennsylvanian was not yet ready to set aside his pen — or his bifocals.

I have always set a greater value on the character of a doer of good, than on any other kind of reputation.
—BENJAMIN FRANKLIN

State House on the morning of May 26. And despite the severe pain he was in and the stifling heat of a Philadelphia summer, Franklin was to arrive every day thereafter, without missing a session, up until the day the convention adjourned on September 17.

Although he refrained for the most part from active participation in the contentious debates that raged in the State House that summer, Franklin proved to be invaluable to the success of the convention and the adoption of the Constitution. In an almost paternal fashion, he exerted a continual calming effect over the quarrelsome and frequently short-tempered delegates, and his humor, wisdom, common sense, and goodwill often kept the laborious process from breaking down altogether. His final speech, in which he appealed to the members of the convention to "sacrifice to the public good" their own personal objections to the Constitution and adopt it unanimously, was perhaps Franklin's greatest act of diplomacy, for in persuading this fractious group of provincial leaders to affix their signatures to the Constitution, it helped turn an alliance of 13 separate states into a unified whole —a nation.

Following the Constitutional Convention, Franklin began to withdraw from public service, content to rest and watch from the sidelines. He was now confident that a great future lay ahead for the United States, and he was satisfied for the most part with the direction the country was taking politically and economically. However, there was one issue that troubled him deeply. Like a small number of other observers, Franklin had realized that the existence of slavery in the United States contradicted the very principles on which the new nation was founded — liberty and equality — and he believed that unless the problem was addressed it would eventually undermine the peace and well-being of America.

Franklin had once been a minor slaveholder himself, but in the course of his lifetime he had come to recognize slavery for what it was — a social and moral abomination. He began to take an active role in the abolitionist movement in the United States,

and soon he was at the forefront of the Pennsylvania effort, as president of the Pennsylvania Society for Promoting the Abolition of Slavery. Because Franklin was frequently too ill to venture outdoors, the society often gathered in his bedroom, where, in February 1789, Franklin wrote and signed the first remonstrance against slavery addressed to Congress. A congressional committee considered the petition, but ruled that slavery was legally a matter for the separate states, and decided that Congress had no authority to interfere in the internal affairs of the states.

Founding Fathers George Washington and Benjamin Franklin meet in private after a session of the Constitutional Convention. Franklin's presence had a continual calming effect over the combative proceedings. "We are here to *consult*, not to *contend*," he advised the delegates.

On September 17, 1787, 39 delegates to the Philadelphia Convention signed the Constitution. Franklin, who can be seen on the left, said on that occasion that "the longer I live the more convincing proofs I see that God governs in the affairs of men."

Although Congress had neatly sidestepped the troublesome issue, Franklin was undaunted. Once again exercising a keen foresight into the future of the country, Franklin raised the issue of the fate of freed slaves, who were uneducated and unprepared to assume a role in society. In an address to the public on November 9, 1789, he stated that "Slavery is such an atrocious debasement of human nature, that its very extirpation, if not performed with solicitous care, may sometimes open a source of serious evils." Therefore, Franklin asserted, it was necessary for those who worked for the abolition of slavery to try to provide education, advice, and employment for freed slaves and to provide for their children as well.

By 1790, Franklin's health was deteriorating rapidly. His intellectual capacity remained undiminished, however, and his wit was as sharp as ever. His last published writing was an appropriately satirical attack on a proslavery speech given by James Jackson, a Georgia representative in Congress. In this article, published in the *Federal Gazette* in the spring of 1790, Franklin compared Jackson's defense of the slave trade — in which the Georgian stated that the morality of slavery was uncertain but that the economic necessity of slave labor in the South was absolutely clear — to a fictional speech by a supposed "North African." The latter, Franklin alleged, had argued a hundred years earlier for the enslavement of white Christians, using reasons that paralleled Jackson's. By showing that the reasoning of Jackson's speech could be used equally well against whites, Franklin exposed it as ridiculous.

Although Franklin's essay failed to move Congress — a second antislavery petition also had no effect — it marked a fitting end to the career of Franklin the political satirist. Had he lived another 70 years, Franklin would have been appalled to see his worst fears about slavery come true, as the Union he and his contemporaries had worked so hard to achieve was divided in bloody civil war.

Franklin spent his final days in the house on Market Street, where he lived — in a separate wing that had been built upon his return from France — with his daughter and her family. Franklin's part of the house included a large dining room and a library. (His personal collection of more than 4,000 books was one of the largest and best in the nation.) The

A Virginian, his daughter at his side, oversees the work of the slaves on his plantation. Unlike many of his contemporaries, Franklin deplored slavery and predicted — correctly — that it would bring disaster to the Union.

library also contained his two final inventions: an instrument for taking down books from high shelves — a wooden pole with a mechanism to operate a clamp on the far end that could grab a book securely — and a special library chair, which had a seat that flipped up, exposing a small stepladder that could also be used for reaching books on high shelves.

Franklin continued to work on his autobiography, which he hoped would "benefit the young reader, by showing him my example, and my success in emerging from poverty, and acquiring some degree of wealth, power, and reputation, the advantages of certain modes of conduct which I observed, and of avoiding the errors which were prejudicial to me." Franklin never did complete this final public service, although in its fragmentary form — covering only the first half of his life — the autobiography fulfills his purpose of telling the story of his climb to

A Dutch man-of-war lands its cargo of slaves at Jamestown, Virginia. Franklin's last published writing was a satirical attack on the institution of slavery.

Franklin lived out his final years in a house he shared with his daughter, Sarah Bache, and her family. He spent most of the time there involved in what he called idle pursuits: reading, conversing with friends, and tending his garden.

worldly prominence, setting an ambitious example for the youth of America, who Franklin felt would surely follow in his footsteps.

Although he had been painfully afflicted with bladder stones, it was pleurisy that finally killed Benjamin Franklin, and he died peacefully at home during the evening of April 17, 1790. Franklin had made a will in 1788, leaving the bulk of his estate to his daughter Sarah and her family, with smaller bequests to the two grandsons who had been with him in Paris, William Temple Franklin and Benjamin Bache. Citing "the part he played against me in the late war," Franklin took his resentment of his eldest son to the grave; William was left virtually nothing. In a late addition to the will, the eternally civic-minded Franklin made donations to the cities of Boston and Philadelphia, which had been the sites of his growth and maturity and where he had been given opportunities to improve himself. He was buried on April 21 at Christ Church in Philadelphia, next to his wife Deborah and his son Francis. Twenty thousand mourners turned out for his funeral.

It is fitting that Franklin left behind an unfinished autobiography: Always the humorist, it is as if he was playing a final joke on those who would

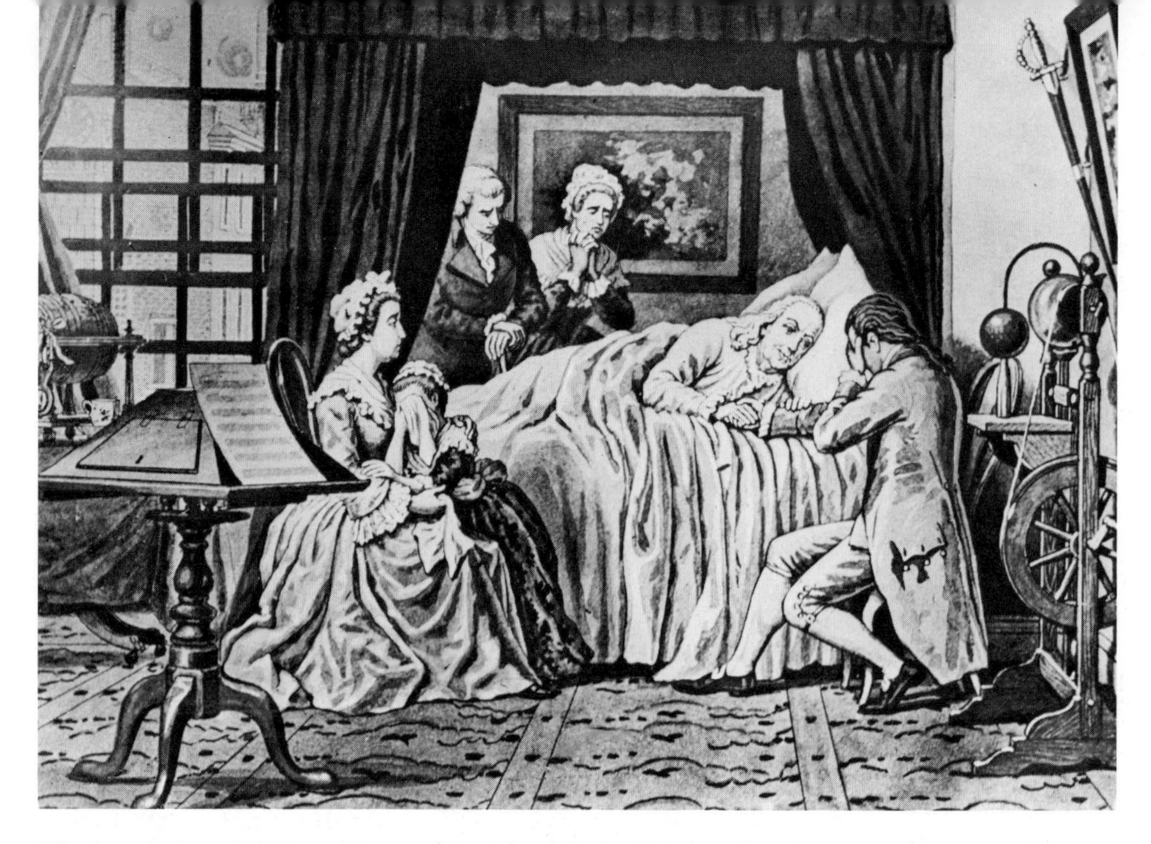

The ever-cheerful Franklin, on his deathbed, bids goodbye to a grieving friend. Franklin wrote that he would meet his imminent death with "little Regret, as, having seen during a long life a good deal of this world, I feel a growing curiosity to be acquainted with some other."

have had him draw definite conclusions about his own life and character; always elusive during his life, he remains so in death.

Admired by many for his practicality, his wisdom, his humor, and his dedication to the public good, Franklin is disliked by others for what they see as his materialism, cunning, hedonism, and lack of imagination. Many of his peers, and later critics such as writers Herman Melville and Mark Twain, have severely criticized Franklin for what they consider his small-minded obsession with moneymaking, his tendency to make petty rules for living, and his preoccupation with foolish gadgetry and inventions. Others have praised Franklin for his realistic attitude toward practical matters and his disdain for useless abstractions. Franklin would agree that he did not have Thomas Jefferson's charisma, Alexander Hamilton's intellectual brilliance, or Thomas Paine's revolutionary fervor. But Franklin's wisdom, worldliness, adaptability, and sense of justice more than compensated for his shortcomings and allowed him to make contributions that are the equal of those made by his illustrious contemporaries.

Benjamin Franklin's greatest contribution was not made in the laboratory, in pamphlets and almanacs, in Congress, or at the negotiating table. It was made, rather, in the way he lived, in the way he created, virtually from nothing, a life that stands as the model of the American success story. From humble colonial beginnings, Franklin eventually became one of the most widely known and respected men in the world, and his rise to greatness and prestige paralleled the rise of the United States. As a symbol of the potential of the new America, Benjamin Franklin has no equal: He was the embodiment of the promise of opportunity that the United States held out to the common man.

Benjamin Franklin passed away quietly on April 17, 1790, at the age of 84. He had written his own epitaph years earlier: "The body of B Franklin, Printer, Lies here, Food for Worms. But the Work shall not be lost; For it will appear once more, in a new and more elegant Edition, Revised and corrected *By the Author*."

Further Reading

Bruns, Roger. *George Washington.* New York: Chelsea House, 1987.

———. *Thomas Jefferson.* New York: Chelsea House, 1986.

Clark, Ronald. *Benjamin Franklin: A Biography.* New York: Random House, 1983.

Cohen, I. Bernard. *Benjamin Franklin: Scientist and Statesman.* New York: Scribners, 1975.

Cousins, Margaret. *Ben Franklin of Old Philadelphia.* New York: Random House, 1963.

D'Aulaire, Ingri, and Edgar P. Parin. *Benjamin Franklin.* New York: Doubleday, 1987.

Dull, Jonathan R. *A Diplomatic History of the American Revolution.* New Haven: Yale University Press, 1985.

Dwyer, Frank. *John Adams.* New York: Chelsea House, 1989.

Franklin, Benjamin. *The Autobiography of Benjamin Franklin.* Edited by J. A. Lemay. New York: Norton, 1986.

Hanna, William S. *Benjamin Franklin & Pennsylvania Politics.* Stanford, CA: Stanford University Press, 1964.

Lancaster, Bruce. *The American Revolution.* Boston: Houghton Mifflin, 1985.

Lemay, J. A., ed. *The Oldest Revolutionary: Essays on Benjamin Franklin.* Philadelphia: University of Pennsylvania Press, 1976.

Paine, Thomas. *Common Sense.* New York: Penguin, 1982.

Schlesinger, Arthur M., jr. *The Birth of a Nation: A Portrait of the American People on the Eve of Independence.* Boston: Houghton Mifflin, 1988.

Wright, Esmond. *Fabric of Freedom: 1763–1800.* New York: Hill & Wang, 1978.

———. *Franklin of Philadelphia.* Cambridge: Harvard University Press, 1988.

Chronology

Jan. 20, 1706	Born Benjamin Franklin in Boston
1718	Serves as printer's apprentice to brother James
1722	"Silence Dogood" essays published anonymously in *New England Courant*
1723	Franklin leaves Boston for Philadelphia
1724–26	Sails for England; works as a printer; returns to America
1729–30	Purchases *Pennsylvania Gazette;* marries Deborah Read
1731	Publishes *Poor Richard's Almanack* (continually until 1758)
1736–37	Founds Union Fire Company; appointed postmaster of Philadelphia
1742–44	Invents the Franklin stove; proposes development of the University of Pennsylvania
1747	Writes *Plain Truth*
1751	*Experiments and Observations on Electricity* is published in London; Franklin founds Pennsylvania Hospital; elected to the Pennsylvania Assembly
1753–54	Appointed deputy postmaster general; helps General Edward Braddock defend Pennsylvania against Indian attacks
1757	Sails to London as representative of Pennsylvania Assembly
1762–64	Returns to America; loses race for Pennsylvania Assembly; returns to London
1766	Testifies on the Stamp Act before House of Commons
1775	Returns to America; elected to Continental Congress; submits Articles of Confederation
1776	Signs Declaration of Independence; sails to France to negotiate alliance
1778	Negotiates and signs Treaty of Alliance and Treaty of Amity and Commerce with France; France declares war on Britain
1782	Franklin negotiates treaty with Great Britain
1785	Returns to Philadelphia; appointed delegate to the Constitutional Convention
1790	Dies in Philadelphia

Index

Account of the New-Invented Pennsylvania Fire-place, An (Franklin), 45
Adams, John, 85, 90, 92–93, 96, 106
Adams, Matthew, 22
Albany Plan of Union, 59
Alger, Horatio, 41
Allen, Ethan, 88
American Revolution, 17, 59, 65, 73, 83–85, 87–97
American Weekly Mercury, 35
Articles of Confederation and Perpetual Union, 83–84
Bache, Benjamin Franklin (grandson), 89, 105
Bache, Richard (son-in-law), 89
Banks, Joseph, 97
Bond, Thomas, 55
Boston, 18, 21, 27–28, 47, 66, 81, 105
Boston Gazette, 23
Boston Massacre, 78
Boston Tea Party, 81
Bradford, Andrew, 28, 35, 45
Bradford, William, 24, 28
Brillon de Jouy, Madame, 93
Bunker Hill, Battle of, 88
Canada, 87–88, 97
Collins, John, 24
Collinson, Peter, 49
Concord, 73
Congress, U.S., 100–103
Constitution, U.S., 13
Constitutional Convention, 13–18, 99–100
Continental Army, 88, 93
Continental Congress, 82–83, 85, 88–89, 97
Cool Thoughts on the Present Situation of Our Public Affairs (Franklin), 70
Cushing, Thomas, 80
Deane, Silas, 89
Declaration of Independence, 13, 85, 87
Delaware, 85
Denham, Thomas, 30–31, 34–35
d'Houdetot, Comtesse, 93
Dissertation on Liberty and Necessity, Pleasure and Pain, A (Franklin), 31, 37
Electricity, 45, 47–54, 57, 77
Enlightenment, 90–91
Experiments and Observations on Electricity (Franklin), 77
Fort Duquesne, 57–58
Fort Ticonderoga, 88
France, 89–97
Franklin, Abiah Folger (mother), 18
Franklin, Benjamin,
    attempts at moral perfection, 40–42
    at Constitutional Convention, 13–18, 99–100
    diplomatic missions of, 61–64, 71, 73–83, 88–97
    early years, 18–25
    favors war with England, 83
    marries, 38
    named postmaster general of United States, 87
    opposes Indian massacres, 68–69
    opposes slavery, 88, 100–103
    opposes Stamp Act, 74–76
    publishes periodicals, 35, 37–42, 45
    scientific work and inventions of, 45–47, 49–54, 57, 77, 104
    serves in Continental Congress, 83–85
    urges colonial unity against French and Indians, 57–59
    works as printer's assistant, 27–35
Franklin, Benjamin (uncle), 19
Franklin, Deborah Read (wife), 28–29, 37–39, 65, 75, 83, 105
Franklin, Ebenezer (brother), 18
Franklin, Elizabeth Downes (daughter-in-law), 65–66
Franklin, Francis (son), 39, 44, 105
Franklin, James (brother), 21–24, 45
Franklin, Josiah (brother), 20
Franklin, Josiah (father), 18, 21–22, 29
Franklin, Sarah (daughter), 39, 65, 89, 91–92, 105
Franklin, William (son), 38, 56, 61–62, 65–66, 71, 79, 84, 105
Franklin, William Temple (grandson), 89, 105
Franklin stove, 45
French and Indian War, 67
French settlers, 57–59
General Magazine and Historical Chronicle, The, 45
George III, king of England, 63, 73–74, 84
Grace, Robert, 45
Great Britain, 13–14, 16, 21, 29, 59, 61–65, 67, 70–71, 73–85, 88–97
"Green Mountain Boys," 88

Grenville, George, 74
Hall, David, 47, 61
Hamilton, Alexander, 106
Harvard University, 20, 56
Helvétius, Madame, 93
Holmes, Robert, 28
Hughes, John, 75
Hutchinson, Thomas, 79–80, 87
Idea of the English School (Franklin), 54
Independence Hall, 13
Intolerable Acts, 81
Iroquois Indians, 59
Jackson, Richard, 70
Jay, John, 96
Jefferson, Thomas, 85, 97, 106
Keimer, Samuel, 28–29, 35
Keith, William, 28–29
Lake Champlain, 88
Lee, Arthur, 89
Lexington, 73, 83
Leyden jar, 50–51, 53
Livingston, Robert, 85
London, 16, 27, 29–31, 37, 61–62, 64, 66, 71, 73, 80–81
Long Island, Battle of, 88
Lord Granville, 62–63
Louis XV, king of France, 76
Louis XVI, king of France, 90, 94
Marie Antoinette, 97
Massachusetts, 77, 79, 81–82
Mather, Cotton, 23, 45
Melville, Herman, 106
Meredith, Hugh, 35, 45
Mississippi River, 97
Narrative of the Late Massacres, A (Franklin), 69
New England Courant, 23, 45
New Jersey, 43–44, 65–66, 77, 84–85, 88
New York, 24, 61, 85, 88
Oliver, Andrew, 79
Pacificus, 75–76
Palmer, Samuel, 31
Paris, 76, 92, 97
Parliament, 63, 70, 74, 76, 81–82
Passy, France, 90, 92–93
"Paxton Boys," 68–70
Penn, William, 27, 57
Pennsylvania, 39, 54, 57, 59, 70, 75, 85
Pennsylvania Assembly, 56, 61–62, 67, 70–71, 99
Pennsylvania Constitutional Convention, 87
Pennsylvania Gazette, 16, 35, 42–43, 45, 53–55, 58
Pennsylvania Society for Promoting the Abolition of Slavery, 101
Philadelphia, 13–18, 24–25, 27–29, 31–32, 34, 46–47, 50, 54, 62, 65–66, 69–70, 75, 80, 83–85, 87, 99–100, 105
Philadelphia Academy, 54
Philadelphia Hospital, 54–55
Plain Truth (Franklin), 54
Pontiac rebellion, 68
Poor Richard's Almanack, 39–41, 61, 74
Priestly, Joseph, 95
Proposals Relating to the Education of Youth in Pennsylvania (Franklin), 54
Puritans, 18, 21, 23
Quakers, 27, 41, 67, 69
Ralph, James, 30–31
Read, John, 28
Religion of Nature Delineated, The (Wollaston), 31
Rousseau, Jean-Jacques, 93
Royal Society of London, 49, 57
Sherman, Roger, 85
"Silence Dogood," 23
Sons of Liberty, 74
South Carolina, 39, 42, 65, 85
Spencer, Archibald, 47, 49
Stamp Act, 70, 74–76
Stevenson, Margaret, 62, 73, 76
Stevenson, Mary, 62
Strahan, William, 46, 64
Timothee, Louis, 42
Treaty of Alliance, 94
Treaty of Amity and Commerce, 94
Treaty of Paris, 97
Twain, Mark, 41, 106
Union Fire Company, 43
University of Pennsylvania, 54
Valley Forge, 93
Vergennes, Comte de, 89, 94
Washington, George, 17–18, 88, 94
Whitmarsh, Thomas, 39
Wilcox, John, 31
Wilson, James, 17
Wollaston, William, 31
Yale University, 56
Yorktown, Battle of, 96

Christopher Looby holds an M.A. in American literature and history from Washington University, St. Louis and a Ph.D. from Columbia University, New York. His essays on Benjamin Franklin have appeared in *Eighteenth Century Studies* and *American Quarterly*. A former associate editor for The Library of America, he currently teaches English at the University of Chicago.

Arthur M. Schlesinger, jr., taught history at Harvard for many years and is currently Albert Schweitzer Professor of the Humanities at City University of New York. He is the author of numerous highly praised works in American history and has twice been awarded the Pulitzer Prize. He served in the White House as special assistant to Presidents Kennedy and Johnson.

PICTURE CREDITS

Atwater Kent Museum: p. 66; Bettmann Archive: pp. 12, 19, 36, 51, 58, 60, 65, 67, 71, 80, 82, 85, 86, 90, 93, 102, 106, 107; Bettmann/Hulton: p. 33; Bostonian Society: p. 81; Culver Pictures: pp. 25, 26, 30, 45, 47, 55, 105; Mary Evans Picture Library: pp. 32, 34, 63; J. L. G. Ferris/Archives of '76/ Bay Village, Ohio: p. 16; Giraudon/Art Resource: pp. 92, 96; Library of Congress: USZ62-1434, p. 2, USZ62-48878, pp. 14–15, USZ62-21242, p. 20, USZ62-17881, p. 22, LCD-407, p. 24, USZ62-2583, p. 29, p. 38, USZ62-17879, p. 40, USZ62-38375, p. 41, USZ62-9844, p. 42, USZ62-54187, p. 44, USZ62-17880, p. 46, USZ62-21623, p. 48, D416-28051, p. 52, USZ62-051691, pp. 56–57, USZ62-15553, p. 64, USZ62-42285, p. 68, USZ62-047286, p. 69, USZ62-10196, p. 70, USZ62-2062, p. 72, LC-D401, p. 74, USZ62-1505, p. 77, USZ62-2141, pp. 78–79, USZ62-8623, p. 84, USZ62-13979, p. 89, USZ62-45183, p. 91, USZ62-58560, p. 95, USZ62-58558, p. 97, USZ62-52063, p. 98, USZ62-35376, p. 103, USZ62-53345, p. 104; New York Historical Society: pp. 94, 101